Fundamentals of Cybersecurity

DANTES/DSST* Study Guide

All rights reserved. This Study Guide, Book and Flashcards are protected under the US Copyright Law. No part of this book or study guide or flashcards may be reproduced, distributed or stored in a retrieval system, or transmitted in any form or by any means, electronic, mechanical, photocopying, recording, or otherwise, without the prior written permission of the publisher Breely Crush Publishing, LLC.

© 2019 Breely Crush Publishing, LLC

DSST is a registered trademark of The Thomson Corporation and its affiliated companies, and does not endorse this book.

9711091518143

Copyright ©2003 - 2019, Breely Crush Publishing, LLC.

All rights reserved.

This Study Guide, Book and Flashcards are protected under the US Copyright Law. No part of this publication may be reproduced, distributed or stored in a retrieval system, or transmitted in any form or by any means, electronic, mechanical, photocopying, recording, or otherwise, without the prior written permission of the publisher Breely Crush Publishing, LLC.

Published by Breely Crush Publishing, LLC
10808 River Front Parkway
South Jordan, UT 84095
www.breelycrushpublishing.com

ISBN-10: 1-61433-596-6
ISBN-13: 978-1-61433-596-2

Printed and bound in the United States of America.

*DSST is a registered trademark of The Thomson Corporation and its affiliated companies, and does not endorse this book.

Table of Contents

Applications & Systems Security 1
    Best Practices for Bringing New Services and Applications in Production 1
    Confidentiality, Integrity and Availability (CIA) 3
    Vulnerability, Mitigation, Threat and Other Terminologies 4
    COOP - Warm, Cold, Hot 6
    Implementing and Maintaining Encryption 7
    Application-layer Encryption 8
    SSL/TLS Communication Protocol 9
    Security Concerns, Solutions and SDLC 10
    Phase I Initialization 10
    Phase II Development/Acquisition 11
    Phase III Implementation 12
    Phase IV Maintenance 12

Authentication and Authorization 13
    Implementing Authentication Technologies 13
    Digitally Signing Data and Asymmetric Keys 15
    Authorization 16
    Certificates of Authority and Standards 18
    MAC vs. DAC 19

Compliance & Governance 20
    Security Architecture 20
    Identifying Risks and Threats 21
    The Different Steps of Digital Forensics 23
    Outsources Process Governance 25
    Freedom of Information Act 26
    Ethics and Information Security 27
    Privacy and the Associated Legislation 28
    HIPAA 28
    Sarbanes-Oxley 29
    USA Patriot Act 29
    Digital Millennium Copyright Act (DMCA) 29

Operational Security 30
    Security and Monitoring the Environment 30
    Audit Logs 30
    Securing and Monitoring Cloud and Virtualization 31
    Security in a Cloud 33

  Virtual Private Networks *34*
  Virtual Machines *35*

Network Security *37*
  Network Security Protocols *37*
  Ports *39*
  Network Scanning *40*
  Network Management Analysis *40*
  Cryptography *42*
  WEP/WPA/WPA2 .... *46*
  Firewall/IDS/IPS *48*
  IDS vs. IPS *49*

Physical & Environmental Security *50*
  Physical Security *50*
  Biometrics *51*
  FAR/FRR/FER/Crossover Error Rates *52*
  Media Management *53*
  Environmental Controls *54*
  Fail Safe vs. Fail Secure *55*

Vulnerability Management *56*
  Testing the Network *56*
  Hacker Attacks *57*
  DoS and DDoS *58*
  IAVA/Patching *62*

Sample Test Questions *64*
Test Taking Strategies *95*
Legal Note *95*

APPLICATIONS & SYSTEMS SECURITY

Best Practices for Bringing New Services and Applications in Production

A best practice can be thought as an issue, technique, or mediation which is generally executed or took after by an organization, or an administration body, proficient affiliation, or other legitimate element. As a rule, this is a system or project increases such status by being

- Measurable: Its objectives are clear and that advancement to them can be measured.
- Notably fruitful: The technique or program picks up great results, as well as makes more advancement to attaining its objectives than most others with comparative points.
- Replicable: The technique or system is organized and reported unmistakably enough so it can be duplicated.

The best practices related to information security for bringing new IT services or applications in organizations can be viewed with different perspectives.

As per the perspective of general management, the IT managers throughout the organizations should consider information security as a normal part of their responsibility. They should clearly define and assign different information security rules and the responsibilities. There should be ensured that sufficient resources are allocated for these. Whenever a new application or a new service is installed, the creation, enforcing and regular reviewing of security policies attached to it is very important.

Another main category of best practices exercised are by creating appropriate policies. We should always develop, deploy and try to enforce security policies that satisfies business objectives. Policies should address key security topic issues such as security risk management, critical asset identification, various physical security issues, systems and network management, authentication and authorizations, access controls, and privacy.

We have to ensure that each and every application or service that is implemented in a secure network environment is covered with these policies and the intention of the policy should be reflected in the standards, procedures, practices and security architectures that implement it.

There should be an efficient risk management routine which periodically conduct information security risk evaluation that identifies: critical information assets, threats to critical assets, asset vulnerabilities and risks and also help to develop and implement a risk mitigation plan resulting from the evaluation.

A security architecture should be generated, implemented, and maintained based on satisfying business objectives and protecting the most critical information assets. The security architecture deployed should have a layered approach, including the practices that follow. It should also use diversity and redundancy solutions for high-risk and high-reliance systems.

All the users of the IT environment, (this include all those who have active accounts, including employees, partners, suppliers, and vendors) should consider information security to be a part of their responsibilities, receive training in all policy topics, and experience consequences related to policy violations.

The other points that should be included in the best practices are:

- Proper access controls, data encryption and virtual private network technologies.
- Removable storage media for critical data.
- Deploying a system discard process that eradicates all data from disks and memory prior to disposal. Use appropriate monitoring, auditing, and inspection facilities and assign responsibility for reporting, evaluating, and responding to system and network events and conditions.
- Regularly use system, networking monitoring tools, filtering and analysis tools, and examine the results.
- Respond to events that warrant action.
- Proper control on physical access to information assets and IT services and resources.

We should use physical access controls where required. Password-controlled electronic locks can be installed for workstations, servers, and laptops that are enabled upon login and after specified periods of activity. Access to all critical hardware assets should be under control.

Confidentiality, Integrity and Availability (CIA)

Information security best practices usually revolve around the CIA triad.CIA refers to confidentiality, integrity and availability. Confidentiality of information, integrity of information and the availability of information are the three important aspects in security. Many security measures are designed to protect one or more facets of the CIA triad.

Confidentiality
The confidentiality of information, basically implies protecting the information from disclosure to unauthorized parties.

Information has a great value, especially in today's world. Information regarding bank account statements, personal information, credit card numbers, trade secrets, government documents, etc., are examples of that information that should be kept as confidential or secure. Protecting such information is a very major part of information security.

The key component of protecting information confidentiality is encryption. Encryption ensures that only the right people (people who knows the key) can read the information. Encryption is widespread in today's environment and can be found in almost every major protocol in use. The stable protocol SSL/TLS, that is used as a security protocol for communications over the internet is one among the best examples. It uses high encryption standards and has been used along with a large number of internet protocols to ensure security.

Other ways to ensure information confidentiality include enforcing file permissions and access control list to restrict access to sensitive information in various FTP servers and application servers.

Integrity
Integrity of information refers to protecting information from being modified by unauthorized parties. The information only has value if it is correct. Information that has been tampered with could prove costly. The integrity of information should be guarded in the case of online transactions and other data-in-transit. As with data confidentiality, cryptography plays a very important role in ensuring data integrity. Integrity breach is very common when the data is being transferred.

The most commonly used methods to protect data includes hashing the data you receive and comparing it with the hash of the original message. However, this means that the hash of the original data must be provided to you in a secure fashion. More convenient methods would be to use digitally signatures to sign the data.

Availability
Availability of information refers to ensuring that authorized parties are able to access the information when needed.

Information only has value if the right people can access it at the right times. Denying access to information has become a very common attack. The Denial of Service attacks or DoS is an attack in which the legitimate user is denied service of any particular application of access for any data. DDoS is distributed denial of services. The primary aim of DDoS attacks is to deny users of the website access to the resources of the website. Such downtime can be very costly. Other factors that could lead to lack of availability to important information may include accidents such as power outages or natural disasters such as floods.

We can ensure data availability by employing efficient backup schemes. Regularly doing off-site backups can limit the damage caused by damage to hard drives or natural disasters. For information services that is highly critical, redundancy might be appropriate.

Vulnerability, Mitigation, Threat and Other Terminologies

There are various terminologies used in information security. The main terminologies that we encounter with are vulnerability, mitigation, vulnerability assessment, and threat.

All these terms can be considered under the common umbrella term risk management. Risk management best practices is something which is un avoidable in any business organization. In perspective of IT, risk management deals all those activities which directly or indirectly affect the CIA triad of information security (Confidentiality, Integrity, Availability).These terminologies can further be defined and explained as follows.

Threat: This term defines or refers to those elements that might attack against.ie what assets, may get attacked, using what resources the attacks can be, what would be the goal of the attacker in mind, when/where/why, and with what probability. The threat definitions might also be included some general aspect of the nature of the attack, but not details about the attack or the security measures that must be defeated and the vulnerabilities to be exploited.

Threat Assessment (TA): This is the assessment done, as an attempt to predict possible threats. This may involve using intelligence data and information on past security incidents. Various incidents of data thefts, intrusion detection and other security breaches can also be studied. The main aim of this assessment to have a proactive security against all the threats that can be caused.

Vulnerability: A vulnerability can be defined as a specific weakness in security (or a lack of security measures) that typically could be exploited by multiple adversaries having a range of motivations and interest in a lot of different assets.

Vulnerability Assessment (VA): Vulnerability assessment is a practice that is executed attempting to discover (and perhaps demonstrate) security vulnerabilities that could be exploited by an intruder. A good vulnerability assessment would often suggests practical countermeasures or improvements in security to eliminate or mitigate the vulnerability, or to aid in resiliency and recovery after an attack.

Risk Management: Risk management, is an umbrella term which includes all those practices attempting to minimize security hazards by deciding intelligently how to deploy, modify, or re-assign security resources. This includes all the threat assessments and vulnerability assessments results, the list of all those assets to be protected, consequences of successful attacks, and the resources like time, funding, personnel that is available to provide security.

Attack: An attempt by an adversary to cause harm to valuable assets, usually by trying to exploit one or more vulnerabilities. The harm may include theft, sabotage, destruction, espionage, tampering, or adulteration.

Below given examples can further distinguish between the various threats and vulnerabilities involved:

- Threat: Intruders might install malware in various servers so they can steal social security numbers for purposes of identity theft.

- Vulnerability: The servers do not have up to date virus definitions for their anti-malware software.

- Threat: Thieves could break into our facility and steal our equipment.

- Vulnerability: The lock we are using on the building doors is easy to pick or bump.

- Threat: Nefarious insiders might release confidential information to adversaries.

- Vulnerability: Employees don't currently have a good understanding of what information is sensitive/confidential and what is not, so they can't do a good job of protecting it.

- Threat: Disgruntled employees could sabotage our facility.

- Vulnerability: The organization lacks effective insider threat countermeasures like background checks and disgruntlement mitigation.

Threat mitigation and compliance services are those best practices that can help you get more from your security investment by reducing the cost and complexity of recovering your networks after the occurrence of an attack. The solutions department helps identify IT threats and risks across your organization by leveraging the latest vulnerability and threat intelligence.

COOP - Warm, Cold, Hot

In case of a disruptions or disaster, it is best to have a disaster recovery plan or a business resumption plan. However, many critical businesses cannot afford a breakdown or a disaster and must be continuously continued. To some businesses this means a loss of even minutes means revenue loss which is irrecoverable. Examples include a stock trading site or a railway ticket booking site, etc. The continuity of operations "COOP" was thus born out of necessity and is a very important concept.

The COOP concept allows business to have alternative sites where the business can immediately be shifted, either during or immediately after a disaster or a breakdown. Thus, loss is minimized and business continued.

The COOP concept initially audits the critical functions in an organization and understands which are those functions which need continuity of operations. Thus alternate sites are planned and kept ready, to switch over to during a breakdown or a disaster like earthquake, fire, flooding, hurricanes or tornadoes.

There are three types of sites available under the COOP Concept. These are cold sites, warm sites and hot sites.

Hot sites: The hot sites are disaster recovery sites with all necessary equipment, personnel, software and ready to be shifted without a moment's notice in case of failure/breakdown of the main site. The shifting can also be instantaneous. The cost of maintaining a hot site is very high but is generally done for businesses which cannot afford maintenance shutdowns or even breakdowns for even a few minutes.

Cold sites: The cold sites are sites which are basic with just power and connections. In case of a disaster, you can start over at this new location. However there is no data or equipment. In case of disaster you need to relocate and restart operations. You need to add equipment and personnel and it may take time to set up the same. This is much less expensive compared to the hot sites. Companies have cold sites which do not have criticality of operations and does not mind losing business even for a couple of days.

Warm sites: The warm sites are the compromise between hot and cold sites. These are better equipped compared to the cold sites but the switching over time may be in hours instead of days. The location and equipment may be ready, however, it may need to move the personnel and latest backup immediately after a disaster or a breakdown. The cost of maintaining the warm site may also be between the costs of a hot and a cold site. The switching over may take hours or days depending on the company.

Implementing and Maintaining Encryption

Encryption is a necessity that organizations are realizing now. Today, organizations survive because of critical technologies which others don't have. In such an environment, it becomes mandatory to ensure that data is not lost due to theft, copying or hacking. The critical data needs protection and this is where the encryption comes to play.

The encryption of data can be done for two states stored data and transit data.

Data at Rest/Stored Data
Data is encrypted and saved in disks and other storage media. The encryption ensures that even if the drive is lost or stolen, the data cannot be retrieved without the proper means of decryption. Database encryption can be used to encrypt data at rest or stored data.

Transit Data
Data which is transferred from one location to another also has high potential of being hacked or lost. To overcome these issues data is encrypted before sending and the receiver can open the data only if he has the unique key for the encryption. Again there are different types of encryption methods for transit data.

Algorithms

There are two types of cryptographic algorithms.

- Symmetric Key Cryptosystems: uses the same key to encrypt and decrypt the moving data.
- Asymmetric Key Cryptosystems (Public Key Cryptography): uses two different key cryptosystems. For example, one key for encrypting data communications and the second key for decrypting data.

For the data at rest or stored data, there are various types of data encryption methods. One important encryption standard that exists is application layer encryption. The technique most commonly used are data encryption methods like RSA, AES, etc.

 Application-layer Encryption

Application-layer encryption is actualized by the application that uses the database to store data. The majority of the applications normally scramble information before it is sent to the database. The information is then unscrambled it when retrieved from the database.

The information and encryption keys are not put away in the database and consequently there is no probability of abuse. This is favorable element for this kind of encryption. The level of encryption is dictated by the software engineer of the application. This kind of encryption is these days not utilized much due to numerous downsides. With all that said, this strategy for encryption has dropped out of support with everything except the most security-aware of organizations on the grounds that it has a few genuine disadvantages.

It is very difficult to retrofit encryption at the application layer into a legacy application; each database read and compose operation (SQL inquiry) must be modified to utilize encryption, generally at huge cost from developer time and testing. Also, indexing doesn't work with encoded information; as the scrambled yield is arbitrary, the requesting of scrambled information components will be too.

Lastly, encrypted data is typically stored in binary format, meaning the tables need to be reconstructed to accept binary inputs instead of traditional text, date or monetary values. Hence, application-layer encryption offers the greatest degree of security at the highest cost in complexity and implementation time.

Data in transit can be made secured by using certain communication protocols.

 SSL/TLS Communication Protocol

SSL was originally developed by Netscape. SSLv3 was designed with public review and input from industry. Then, the TLS working group was formed within IETF (internet Engineering Task Force) and published TLSv1.0 that is very close to SSLv3 and can be viewed as SSLv3.1. Later, TLSv1.1 which is a minor modification of TLSv1.0, was proposed.

The "socket layer" exists between the application layer and the transport layer in the TCP/IP protocol stack.

SSL/TLS contains two layers of protocols.

The first layer contains, SSL Record Protocol which provides basic security services to various higher layer protocols and defines the format used to transmit data. SSL defines three higher-layer protocols that use the SSL Record Protocol.

These three protocols are used in the management of SSL exchanges.

- **Change Cipher Spec Protocol:** which updates the cipher suite to be used on SSL connection.
- **Alert Protocol:** Used to convey SSL-related alerts to the peer entity.
- **Handshake Protocol:** This is the most complex part of SSL and is used as a secured transport service.

An SSL connection is a transport service that provides a peer-to-peer type of service. SSL connections are temporary and each connection is associated with one SSL session. An SSL session can be thought of as an association that is created by the Handshake Protocol.

The session defines a set of cryptographic security parameters that can be shared among multiple connections. Once a session is established, there is a "current" operating state for both message receiving and sending."Pending" read and write states are created during the handshaking. Then, upon a successfully completed handshake, pending states become the current states. The SSL record protocol provides the services of confidentiality and data integrity for SSL connections.

On transmission, the SSL record protocol takes an application message, fragments it into manageable blocks, optionally compresses the data, applies a message authentication code, encrypts using a conventional encryption scheme, adds a header, and finally transmits the resulting unit in TCP segments. On other end, received data are decrypted, verified, decompressed, reassembled, and then delivered to the users.

Security Concerns, Solutions and SDLC

SDLC or software development lifecycle is tailored by the various software engineering concepts that ensure a professional way of product development.

The main objectives of such a principle can be formulated as follows:

- A well formulated requirement specification. This includes both functional and non-functional requirements.
- The software development should be well oriented and organized. The various stages involved in this are planning, development, usage and maintenance.
- Well defined software development models.

The software development lifecycle basically follows a four staged process. This is more of a generic overview since the number of stages and phases can be increased depending upon the selection of different software engineering models.

Some of the common SDLC models are waterfall model, prototype model, evolutionary model, the spiral model and so on. The different phases of SDLC are

- Requirement gathering and analysis
- Design
- Implementation/coding
- Testing
- Deployment
- Maintenance

When we look at these development phases on a security perspective, we have to keep into mind the various security aspects that should be followed in each of these stages. To explain more we can look at each and every development phase of a SDLC and suggest appropriate security measures for each of these phases.

Phase I Initialization

This phase comprises of requirement gathering and analysis. The existing system or process is reviewed along with the new requirement needs. A proper analysis of the proposed requirements is made. The main deliverables of this phase includes

- Funding requests
- Project plan
- Cost benefit analysis
- User requirements

All these are included in the detailed SRS (Software Requirement Specification) document. The various security measures that can be incorporated in this phase are

- Risk assessment, including a data sensitivity assessment can be carried out which includes a review of all information, potential damage, laws and compliances, threats, security characteristics etc.
- Potential weaknesses towards the information confidentiality, integrity and availability can be singled out.
- Overall security functional requirements and security design considerations can be documented.

Phase II Development/Acquisition

This is the phase where the system is designed, coded or developed. The key deliverables of this phase are:

- Functional and technical requirements
- System test plans
- Security test plans

Here the various functional requirements addresses the different quality assurance requirements, configuration management, etc. The various technical requirements contain performance requirements, interfaces, data characteristics, user screens, other security design concerns, failure scenarios, etc. The various security activities that can occur during this phase are:

- Reviewing the technical features like volume projections, system capabilities and vulnerabilities and the overall system responsiveness.
- Reviewing the various operational practices that are been designed for ensuring operational security. Various security measures can be recommended so that the data and the system components are not compromised. Periodical security audits are also planned accordingly.
- Various test plans and scripts are also reviewed.

# Phase III Implementation

In this phase the system is moved into the production. Here if things go wrong, it can cause additional expenditures and unusual delays and hence low performance. The critical activities carried out in this phase are final testing, system certifying and system installation. The deliverables include the security certification package, user documentation, training materials, contingency plans and the disaster recovery plan.

The various security activities during this phase are

- Developing test data.
- All the three (unit, module and integrative) testing types should be done in a proper manner. This is very important to avoid bugs and other security vulnerabilities.
- Ensuring that the system has gone through proper technical evaluation and that the system compliance with all the laws and regulations.

# Phase IV Maintenance

Maintenance phase deals with the various enhancements and up gradations of the system. The primary concern of this phase is system availability. The various ongoing activities like performance monitoring and managing feedback, managing system problems, implementing the various system changes all comes under this phase.

The various security measures that may be suggested for this phase are

- Reviewing backup and restore parameters
- Performing backups
- Management of cryptographic keys
- Management of user administration and access privileges

AUTHENTICATION AND AUTHORIZATION

Implementing Authentication Technologies

Implementation of various authentic technologies is very essential to ensure the overall security of computer system. Authentication is the enforcing part of the two staged access control process. Authentication technology or mechanisms do differ while authenticating real people or machines. Which authentication of machines relies mostly on private public key, digital signature mechanisms which we cannot really use for authentication of humans.

Authenticating with something we know is the most common method of authentication system that is used. Using of passwords is one of the most common example for these type of authentications. The major threat involved in using this kind of method is that, something we know is something that can be forgotten. Writing or recording our password for not forgetting may cause someone else to find it.

Other threats involved are shoulder surfing which causes the eavesdropper see the secret being typed or wire tapping through which the secret key is incepted through the wire used to send it to the machine. Another problem that may arise is the tendency of the people to select something which can be remembered. This also makes this password easily guessable. Even if a password is not so easy to find, this may be found by an offline search to the password space.

From a users point of view, the major characteristics that can considered for a strong password are

- Length. Increasing the length of the password is the easiest way to make the password stronger.
- Character set. The more characters that can be used in a password, the greater the number of possible combinations of characters, so the larger the password space. Use of capital letters, numeric and alphanumeric value also strengthens the password.
- Randomness. Randomness of the phrase should be increased, so that it is difficult for the attacker to guess.

Storing passwords is another important area that should be considered for security. Simply storing the username and passwords in a file is not a good option for keeping the passwords in a system. Converting the various usernames and passwords into hashes also may succumb to possible offline dictionary attacks. This done by the attacker creating hash for every word from dictionary and comparing this to the hash stored if something matches that password is learned.

Another more effective alternative to this is to use salt. Salt is a random number associated with the user which will be added to the user's password. Salt is used in most UNIX implementations. Another more secured version of salt is the secret salt where a small set of possible secret salt values is selected from a large space. Now the password file for each user is been stored as user id, h(password, public salt, secret salt), public salt. The effect is to make computing a hashed password very expensive for attackers.

Some of the widely-used password systems are

- Unix: Unix stores a hashed salted password and salt.
- FreeBSD: FreeBSD stores a hashed password here, the hash is based on MD5.
- OpenBSD: OpenBSD does a hash based on blowfish encryption, and then stores the hashed password along with 128 bits of salt. The system guarantees that no two accounts will have the same salt value.
- Windows NT/2000/XP: NT stores two password hashes: one called the LanMan hash and another called the NT hash.

As an alternative to passwords, you may use an external device or fob to authenticate. The major authentication technologies in this category are:

Magnetic strip card. A credit card lies in this category. Here this cards are further secured by implementing a 2-factor authentication by keeping a 4 to 7 character PIN whenever the card is used.

Proximity card or RFID. These cards transmit stored information to a monitor via RF. Retail chains like Walmart attaches RFID tags on every product they shelve in order to avoid shoplifting, where as both the German and U.S. governments are including them in passports.

There are two types of RF proximity cards: passive and active.

- Passive RFID are not powered, and hence use the RF energy from the requester to reply with whatever information is being stored by the card.
- Active RFID is powered and hence broadcasts information, allowing anyone who is in range and has a receiver to query the card.

Challenge/response cards and cryptographic calculators. These are called smart cards and perform some sort of cryptographic calculation. These are generally used as an employee id smart card that is used for attendance punching in and out. The card may have memory, and it may even have an associated PIN. Another form of smartcard that are widely in use are RSA secure ids. This type of card continuously displays encrypted time and each and every RSA secure id encrypts with a different key.

Biometrics are the authentication systems based on the biological traits or the physical and behavioral properties you possess.

Some examples include:

- Retinal scan
- Fingerprint reader
- Handprint reader
- Voice print
- Keystroke timing
- Signature

To implement a biometric authentication scheme some representation for the characteristic of interest is stored. Subsequently, when authenticating that person, the characteristic is measured and compared with what has been stored. An exact match is not expected, nor should it be because of error rates associated with biometric sensors.

Constraints for using this type of system include:

- Reliability of the method. Similarity of physical features and inaccuracy of measurement may together may fail the authentication.
- Cost and availability.
- Unwillingness or inability to interact with biometric input devices.
- Compromise the biometric database or system.

Digitally Signing Data and Asymmetric Keys

A digital signature is an authentication system used to authenticate a digital message or document. This is a mathematical scheme or a cryptographic key used for demonstrating that the message is authentic i.e., it is created by its sender. This also equips the recipient with the ability to prove the identity of the sender, even if he denies sending it. Digital signatures are usually used in financial transactions and software distributions.

The digital signature schemes usually employs a type of PKI or asymmetric cryptography for its operation. The public-key cryptography is also called the "asymmetric" due to the asymmetry in key information held by the parties. Here a pair of keys is there during the whole process: a private key (secret key) and another a public key that matches this secret key. The message is encrypted by the sender using the public key at the source and is communicated to the recipient. The recipient (owner of the public/private key pair) decrypts this using his private key at the receiving end.

A digital signature scheme consists of three algorithms that should be performed in the same order as given;

- A key generation algorithm that selects a private key uniformly at random from a set of possible private keys. This algorithm outputs the private key and a corresponding public key.
- A signing algorithm which produces a signature with the given message and a private key.
- A signature verifying algorithm that, given a message, public key and a signature, either accepts or rejects the message's claim to authenticity.

Majorly digital signatures should possess two main properties for its successful operations.

1) The authenticity of a signature generated from a fixed message and fixed private key should be verified by the corresponding public key.
2) They should be impossible to computationally generate a valid signature for a party without knowing that party's private key.

A digital signature is an authentication mechanism that enables the creator of message to attach a code that act as a signature. It is formed by taking the hash of message and encrypting the message with creator's private key.

Authorization

Authorization means giving special rights to a person to access something. This term is often used in computer and information security domain. In fact, authorization is about giving special access rights to otherwise restricted resources. The word to authorize basically means to define an access policy.

Access control rules or policies are formulated taking into consideration various aspects and the access for different resources is given. These resources include individual files, databases, various devices server rooms and various computer applications. In networks, security access control majorly relies on access policies.

In computing systems, authorization can be defined as a process which determines what permissions a user or the system should have. In system that has more than one user, different groups of users are given different rules or privileges Mostly this is decided by a system administrator. Privileges includes access to file directories the amount of storage space that can be used, whether the internet access is given or not etc.

An access control process can be seen as a two stage process:

- Formulating phase: here the various permissions or privileges for different users are decided.

- Enforcement phase: where the different policies formulated are checked and decided accordingly, in order to give the access or not.

Authorization happens in the first part of the access control process where the policies are formulated and set for the different categories of users.

The second phase of the access control is done by various user authentication methods. In fact, whether you are authorized to work in an office or not is decided by the management of the company and an employee id is created for you. But the authentication process only happens when you swipe your ID card in order to get the access inside your office.

The various types of authorization services used in giving authorization for uses in a typical computer system are

- Active directory security groups can be thought of as an effective way to provide very strict authorization lists. In other words, here a particular group is been given access to a resource or a service and not a list of users. Here the network ID pass phrase is looked up by the ADS to check whether the user is a member of that security group or not in order to grant the access.

- Apache require is another authorization method that selects which authenticated users can access a particular resource. Here this process executes after the authentication phase is over. This method relies largely on a locally maintained list of users or groups to decide whether the users that are authenticated is able to access a particular resource or not.

Certificates of Authority and Standards

Certificate authority or a certification authority is a trusted third party entity that issues digital certificates. The digital certificate is used to create digital signatures and also asymmetric, private and public key pairs. This also certifies the ownership of the public key by the named individual or organization. The role of a CA is important for data security and ecommerce because they guarantee that the two parties exchanging data are who they are claim to be. This allows both parties to rely upon the signatures made by the private key that is a part of the certified public key.

The certificates from the trusted CAs are used to securely transfer files with the various servers online. Digital certificates also help avoid the various concerns that can affect the security of data. The common security attack which is a real threat on data security is the man-in-the-middle attack. This is a scenario where a malicious outsider pretends to be the target server and tries to attain control on the data sent originally to the target server. This situation can be avoided, by a client which uses a digital certificate and verifies the signature on the server certificate before setting up a connection for data transfer.

Mostly in the connections through internet, the web browsers usually possess a set of trusted CA certificates. A malicious client can also get away with any security check by skipping it and making its users believe it happened. The digital signature placed on the public key certificate by the CA provides the cryptographic binding between the entity's public key, its name and other information in the certificate, such as a validity period. CA manages the certificate lifecycle, which includes generation and issuance, distribution, renewal and rekey. The CA may delegate the first registration of a subscriber to a registration authority which can act as agents for the CA.

The CA also provides certificate status information by issuing Certificate Revocation Lists (CRLs).

A registration authority (RA) is an entity that is responsible for the identification and authentication of subscribers, but does not sign or issue certificates. The subscriber first generates his or her own public/private key pair. Then they produce proof of identity according to the policy requirements and demonstrates that they hold the private key corresponding to the public key without disclosing the private key. Once the link between a person and a public key is verified, the CA issues a certificate. The CA digitally signs each certificate that it issues with its private key to provide the means for establishing authenticity and integrity of the certificate.

A repository is an electronic certificate database that is available online.

A certification practice statement (CPS) is a statement of the practices which a certification authority employs in issuing and managing certificates. A certificate policy (CP) is a named set of rules that indicates the applicability of a certificate to a particular community and/or class of application with common security requirements.

There are two models of CA architectures. CAs may be linked using two basic architectures or a hybrid of the two: (1) hierarchical (2) cross-certified.

In a hierarchical model, a highest level (or "root") CA is deployed and subordinate CAs may be set up for various business units, domains or communities of interest. The root CA validates the subordinate CAs, which in turn issue certificates to the lower tier CAs or directly to the subscribers. A root CA typically has more stringent security requirements than a subordinate CA.

In an alternative model, cross-certified CAs are built on a "peer-to-peer" model. Rather than deploying a common root CA, the cross-certification model shares trust between CAs that are known to one another. Cross certification is a process in which two CAs certify the trustworthiness of the other's certificates. If two CAs, CA1 and CA2, cross-certify, CA1 creates and digitally signs a certificate containing the public key of CA2 (and vice versa).

That means that users in either CA domain are secure because each CA trusts the other and the subscribers in each domain can trust each other. Cross-certified CAs are not subject to the single point of failure in the hierarchical model. In the cross-certified model, establishing and maintaining a community of trust is very important and audits may be performed to make sure that each cross-certified CA conforms to a agreed practices.

MAC vs. DAC

In a multiple user environment, it is very important to ensure that people should only access what they need, proper restrictions should be placed in order to ensure this. Mandatory access control (MAC) and discretionary access control (DAC) are two of the popular access control models that are used for this. The main difference between them is in how they provide access to users.

In MAC, administrators creates a set of levels and each user is linked with a specific access level. The access is restricted for that user for all the resources that are greater than his access level. Whereas in DAC, each resource is assigned with a list of users who can access it. That means the access in DAC is provided based on the identity of the user and not by permission level.

MAC is easier to establish and maintain access for the users, especially when dealing with a great number of users, since you only need to establish a single level for each resource and one level for each user. With DAC, you need to assign the permission level to each and every user. If you have a level 2 user who needs access to a single level 1 resource, with DAC you cannot provide access to that user without giving him access to all other resources in the same category.

But With MAC, you just need to add that user to the list of who can access the resource. It is very easy for system administrators to keep track of who has access to what because they are the only one who can change the permission levels with MAC. DAC provides users who have access to the resource to also provide access to other users by including them in the list which can be problematic. A good example of a MAC is the access levels of Windows for admins, ordinary users, and guests. For DAC, the permissions for Linux file operating systems is a good example.

COMPLIANCE & GOVERNANCE

Security Architecture

A security architecture can be defined as the high level design that gives the structure of the system, which includes identifying main system components, the various defensive measures, and also their secure interconnections. A security domain sets the scope of application of the security architecture.

The security domain is defined as the domain of all the layers of OSI which is a set of network, physical and logical elements protected by the security architecture. The security domain for this particular network system might be considered as the first step to design a security architecture. Clearly, the security domain includes user data link layer communications and the hardware elements being employed at the medium access and link layer that transmit data.

There are various technology and mechanisms that support the security services in the security domain. The security architecture should clearly define the different security technologies and components that are being used for protecting the security domain. This must also include specifying the configuration of the parameters defining each security technology and component being used for this.

The most significant security technology and mechanisms being employed in enterprise security architecture can be listed as follows:

- Cryptographic algorithms like symmetric key (AES, DES, 3DES, IDEA, RC4) used for data confidentiality and integrity.
- Public keys like RSA, ECC are used for entity authentication and symmetric key establishment.
- Digital signatures like RSA, ECC, DSS are used for non-repudiation, user or entity authentication.
- Data integrity and authentication is ensured by using MAC, HMAC, CMAC.
- Symmetric key management schemes like Kerberos, RADIUS are used for entity authentication and authorization. Symmetric key establishment also for accounting the key management tool. Radius is used by ISPs for accounting purposes i.e., who used how much and also for access control.
- Public keys like PKI, PGP are used for entity authentication and authorization.
- The various security suits and standards for various network layers includes IEEE 802.1x for link layer ensures authentication and access control. IPsec for network layer, SSL/TLS for transport layer.
- The application security concerns includes protocols like SMTP/MIME for mail, PGP, HTTP and HTTPS.
- Virtual private networks ensures a secure virtual corporate network by leveraging IPSec, SSL and other technologies.
- The various identification techniques like medium access control address in OSI, PHY and MAC layers, IP address in network layer, and port address in transport layer.
- Human identification and authentication technologies like passwords for software and tokens for hardware.
- In access control systems, we have DAC, RBAC in logical access control systems, physical access controls, and firewalls.

All these constitute the major components that should be included in efficient security architecture.

Identifying Risks and Threats

The main requirement of any risk management strategy is the proper knowledge of the information security professionals regarding their organization's information assets. Next it is needed to identify, classify and prioritize them. Once this is done, the risk/threat assessment processes identifies and try to quantify the risks faced by each asset. The identification of risks is a key component of a healthy, secured and robust information framework of any organization. In the absence of this assessment, the organization is literally unable to effectively manage its key risks and demonstrate that their information sources are well in control and is secure.

An effective risk identification process includes:

- The significant risks of information security objectives should be identified by this process.
- All types of risks, associated with major components and controls either directly or indirectly, from all sources, across the entire scope of the organization's activities should be identified and categorized.
- The various risks around opportunities as well as threats, are identified so that the organization's chance for increasing the benefits of these opportunities can be maximized.
- The entire process should be systematic, disciplined and documented, and also methodical and well-organized and should be put in a format that is capable of being communicated and understood by all.

We should also consider focusing on the root causes and influencing factors of risk, both internal and external, as well as its effects and outcomes.

The organization should consider carefully the risk categorization that it adopts. After identifying and performing the preliminary classification of an organization's information assets, and identifying the impending risks that can be originated the analysis phase moves on to an examination of the threats facing the organization.

The realistic threats must be investigated further while the unimportant threats are set aside. If you assume every threat can and will attack every information asset, the project scope quickly becomes so complex it overwhelms the ability to plan.

The threats to information security can broadly be categorized as:

- Compromises to intellectual property: privacy, copyright infringements.
- Various software attacks: virus, worms, macros, denial of service.
- The deviation in quality of service: ISP, power or WAN service issues from service providers.
- Espionage or trespass: unauthorized access or data collection.
- The various forces of nature: fire, flood, earthquake, or lightening.
- Human error or failure: accidents and employee mistakes.
- Information extortion: black mail, information disclosure.
- Missing inadequate or incomplete: loss of access to information systems due to disk drive failure without proper backup and recovery plan organizational policy or planning in place.

- Missing, inadequate, or incomplete controls: network compromised because of no firewall security control.
- Sabotage or vandalism: destruction of systems or information.
- Theft: illegal confiscation of equipment or information.
- Technical hardware failures and errors: equipment failures.
- Technical software failures and errors: bugs, code problems, unknown loopholes.
- Technological obsolescence: antiquated or outdated technologies.

Each of these threat categories should be assessed and prioritized according to its level of effect on the organization. The threat assessment or ranking can be done by answering a few basic questions:

- Which of the threats present a danger to an organization's assets in a given environment?
- Which threats can be a danger to the organization's information?
- What would be the cost involved in order to recover from a successful attack?
- Which of the threats would require the greatest expenditure to prevent?

By answering these questions, you establish a framework for the discussion of threat assessment.

The Different Steps of Digital Forensics

The word forensics deals with the perfect application of highly methodological investigative techniques to present the evidence. In other words, forensics uses science to investigate events. Digital forensics includes the various tasks like preservation, identification, documentation and interpretation of computer media for root/cause analysis for evidentiary measures.

Digital forensics can be defined as:

The use of scientifically derived and proven methods toward the preservation, validation, identification, analysis, interpretation, documentation and presentation of digital evidence derived from digital sources for the purpose of facilitating or furthering the reconstruction of events found to be criminal, or helping to anticipate unauthorized actions shown to be disruptive to planned operations.

The investigative process of digital forensics can be divided various stages or steps. These stages are properly carried out and are well documented.

These steps are collectively known as chain of evidence or chain of custody.

Once the evidence is in the possession of investigators, its movement, storage, and access is well tracked until the resolution of the event or case. This is usually done by the detailed documentation of the collection, storage, transfer, and ownership of collected evidence from the crime scene through its presentation in court. The evidence is then tracked wherever it is located. When the evidence changes hands or is stored, the documentation is also updated.

Preservation. This involves operations that prevents or stops any activities that can damage the various digital information that can be collected. This includes the various operations such as preventing people from using computers during collection, stopping ongoing deletion processes, and choosing the safest way to collect information.

Collection. This stage is involved in finding or collecting digital information that is relevant to the investigation. Basically, the collection stage consists in collecting the various digital information that may be useful or relevant to the investigation that is being carried out.

Examination. This stage consists of an in-depth systematic "search of evidence" relating to the incident for which the investigation is being carried out. It may consist of different log files, various data files containing some specific phrases, timestamps, etc. Authenticating the recovered evidence is another important task of this stage. Here the various evidences that are collected should go through the next stage of authentication.

The forensic team must be able to demonstrate that whatever they have collected is a true and accurate replica of the source evidence material. Hash matching a hard drive in evidence to validate integrity can be accomplished by the use of cryptographic hash tools.

The hash tool takes a variable-length file and creates a single numerical value, usually represented in hexadecimal notation, like a digital fingerprint. By hashing the source file in the hard drive of a computer and the copy, the investigator can assert that the copy is a true and accurate duplicate of the source.

Analysis. The aim of analysis is to draw conclusions based on evidence found during the examination. Indexing of the evidence material is a major component of the analysis phase. During indexing, many investigatory tools are used to create an index of all text found on the drive. This includes data found in deleted files and in file slack space. The index itself can then be used by the investigator to locate specific documents or document fragments. While indexing, the tools typically organize files into categories, such as documents, images, executables, and so forth.

Report the findings. Once the investigators have found a suitable amount of information they can summarize their findings, along with a synopsis of their investigatory procedures, in a report and is submitted it to the appropriate authority.

Even though in digital forensics, the focus is on procedures, in information/cyber security all operations mostly focus on policies. Policies are those documents which provides the managerial guidance for ongoing implementation and operations. Procedures can minimize the probability of an organization losing a legal challenge. Organizations should develop specific procedures, the handling of potential evidentiary material along with guidance on the use of these procedures.

The policy document should specify the following things clearly

- The personnel that would be conducting the investigation
- The people who are authorized for the investigation
- The affidavit-related documents that are required
- The search warrant-related documents that are required
- The digital media that should be seized or taken offline
- The methodology that is to be followed
- The methods required for chain of custody or chain of evidence
- The format of the final report, and to whom it should it be given

The policy document also should be supported by a procedures manual, developed based on the documents used in the investigation, along with guidance from law enforcement or consultants.

Outsources Process Governance

Out sourcing of various IT services can provide an organization to be free of all the time consuming maintenance headaches and also from the deviation from its core functions. Giving away the full control of the supporting services like IT the some outside organization is very critical.

Therefore prior to any outsourcing arrangement, it is very essential to go through all contractual agreements and a careful consideration of risks and the compliance obligations must also should take place.

While selecting an infrastructure service provider, which is a very critical decision, the main points that should be reviewed include a sound design and implementation of information security principles and practices which can be get integrated well with the client organization.

The information security risks and threats that could compromise the integrity, availability and performance of the services that are outsourced can be

- The lack of compliance to legislative obligations, carried at both outsourcing agent and the organization.
- Costly remediation activities to rectify the service capabilities in the event of an information security breach.

In these modern times where cloud computing is gaining its momentum it is very crucial to have compliance policies for outsource services in place. This also should include clear control execution instructions and regulatory standards giving importance to the information security concerns of the organizations. The specific information security exposures that should be considered by a critical infrastructure provider, like a cloud service provider includes:

- Compliance with jurisdictional legislation
- Managing the confidentiality of information
- Assurance on the effectiveness of information security controls in the cloud

Freedom of Information Act

Freedom of Information Act provides the public access to information held by public authorities.

This act has two functions

- The public authorities should publish certain information about their activities.
- The public are entitled to request these information from public authorities (right to information).

Public authorities include government departments, local authorities, the NHS, state schools and police forces. However, it should also be noted that the act does not cover every organization that receives public money. Recorded information includes printed documents, computer files, letters, emails, photographs, and sound or video recordings. The act does not give people access personal information of individuals such as their health records or credit reference file. If a member of the public wants to see information that a public authority holds about them, they should make a subject access request under the Data Protection Act 1998.

 Ethics and Information Security

The rules that govern personal conduct are collectively known as rules of ethics. Security professionals should maintain high levels of ethics. These are not considered rules, but are minimum standards for professional behavior.

Code of Ethics Preamble
Safety of the commonwealth, duty to our principals, and to each other requires that we adhere, and be seen to adhere, to the highest ethical standards of behavior. Therefore, strict adherence to this code is a condition of certification.

Code of Ethics Canons
The Code of Ethics includes the following canons:

- Protect society, the commonwealth, and the infrastructure.
- Act honorably, honestly, justly, responsibly, and legally.
- Provide diligent and competent service to principals.
- Advance and protect the profession.

The Computer Ethics Institute created its own code of ethics. The Ten Commandments of Computer Ethics are as follows:

1. Thou shalt not use a computer to harm other people.
2. Thou shalt not interfere with other people's computer work.
3. Thou shalt not snoop around in other people's computer files.
4. Thou shalt not use a computer to steal.
5. Thou shalt not use a computer to bear false witness.
6. Thou shalt not copy proprietary software for which you have not paid.
7. Thou shalt not use other people's computer resources without authorization or proper compensation.
8. Thou shalt not appropriate other people's intellectual output.
9. Thou shalt think about the social consequences of the program you are writing or the system you are designing.
10. Thou shalt always use a computer in ways that ensure consideration and respect for your fellow humans.

Privacy and the Associated Legislation

Privacy of information has become so important in this modern era. Big data, analytics, and recommender engines all utilize the power of data. Privacy has become one of the hottest topics in information security at the beginning of the 21st century. There are many organizations that collect, swap, and sell personal information as a commodity. Here in this context we understand privacy as a state of being free from unwanted intrusion. Various policies and laws are made and enforced to ensure this. Some of the relevant privacy laws include the following.

The Privacy of Customer Information Section of the common carrier regulation states that any proprietary information shall be used explicitly for providing services, and not for any marketing purposes, and that carriers cannot disclose this information except when necessary to provide their services. The only other exception is when a customer requests the disclosure of information, and then the disclosure is restricted to that customer's information only.

 HIPAA

The Health Insurance Portability and Accountability Act Of 1996 (HIPAA), also known as the Kennedy-Kassebaum Act, protects the confidentiality and security of health care data by establishing and enforcing standards and by standardizing electronic data interchange. HIPAA affects all health care organizations, including doctors' practices, health clinics, life insurers, and universities, as well as some organizations that have self-insured employee health programs.

HIPAA has five fundamental principles:

1. Consumer control of medical information.
2. Boundaries on the use of medical information.
3. Accountability for the privacy of private information.
4. Balance of public responsibility for the use of medical information for the greater good measured against impact to the individual.
5. Security of health information.

Sarbanes-Oxley

The Sarbanes-Oxley Act of 2002 is a piece of legislation that affects the executive management of publicly traded corporations and public accounting firms. The purpose of this law is to improve the reliability and accuracy of financial reporting while increasing the accountability of corporate governance, in publicly traded companies. Penalties for companies in non-compliance range from a simple fine to time in jail. IT managers are likely to ask information security managers to verify the confidentiality and integrity of those information systems in a process known in the industry as sub-certification.

USA Patriot Act

USA Patriot Act of 2001 provides law enforcement agencies with broader latitude in order to combat terrorism-related activities. In 2006, this act was amended by the USA Patriot Improvement and Reauthorization Act, which made permanent fourteen of the sixteen expanded powers of the Department of Homeland Security and the FBI in investigating terrorist activity. The act also reset the expiration date for certain types of wiretaps under the Foreign Intelligence Surveillance Act of 1978 (FISA), and revised some of the penalties associated with criminal and terrorist activities.

Digital Millennium Copyright Act (DMCA)

The Digital Millennium Copyright Act (DMCA) is the American contribution to an international effort by the World Intellectual Properties Organization (WIPO) to reduce the impact of copyright, trademark, and privacy infringement, especially when accomplished via the removal of technological copyright protection measures. This law was created in response to the 1995 adoption of Directive 95/46/EC by the European Union, which added protection for individuals with regard to the processing of personal data and the use and movement of such data.

The DMCA includes the following provisions:

- Prohibits the removal of protections implemented by the copyright owners to control access to their copyrighted content.
- Prohibits the sale and manufacture of devices manufactured to circumvent protections and countermeasures that control access to protected content.

- Prohibits the altering of information attached to or imbedded in a copyrighted material.
- Excludes internet service providers from certain forms of copyright infringement.

OPERATIONAL SECURITY

Security and Monitoring the Environment

In an organization, proper security of the IT environment is very crucial. In order to effectively secure the network, the first thing is to become familiar with all of the components in it. This also includes identifying all the assets and also monitoring the various security issues that comes along with it. It is also very much necessary to train your IT staff to run periodical security programs.

Proper risk management and threat mitigation programs should also be part of the routine. These vulnerability analysis and also the various risk management practices should be properly documented and a set of security policies should be set. This documentation gives a clear understanding of organizational risk tolerance and set priorities and manage risk consistently throughout the organization. This documentation also

- Includes proper metrics which provides meaningful indications of security status at all organizational tiers.
- The continued effectiveness of all security controls is ensured.
- Verifies compliance with information security requirements derived from various security policies and guidelines.
- To maintain awareness of threats and vulnerabilities.

Audit Logs

An audit log is a full historic account of all events that are relevant for a certain object. In other words, audit logs maintain a record of system activity by system or application processes or by user initiated processes. Therefore audit trails, along with appropriate tools and procedures can help the security professionals in accomplishing solutions to various security concerns.

Audit logs can be effectively used for:

- Accountability of an individual. Audit logs can provide a trace of user actions hence supporting the accountability of the user for that action.
- Audit logs can also be used in the reconstruction of events by supporting after the fact investigations.
- Audit trails can also be used for intrusion detection. Intrusions can be detected in real time, by examining audit records as they are created or after the fact, by examining audit records in a batch process.
- Audit logs are also been used to identify problems as they occur. This is referred to as real-time auditing or monitoring.

An audit log usually contains sufficient information to establish what are the events occurred and who caused them.

An audit log normally specifies

- Type of event: The type of event, and its result is specified. Some examples are failed user authentication attempts, changes to users' security information, organization and application specific security-relevant events.
- When the event occurred: The time and day in which the event occurred is listed here.
- User ID associated with the event: Program or command used to initiate the event.

Securing and Monitoring Cloud and Virtualization

Cloud computing is an emerging area in the field of computer science, that is currently getting momentum in terms of research and implementation with its strong future prospective. Concept wise, it is an encapsulation where the details are hidden from the client who no longer need the knowledge or control over the technology infrastructure that supports them. The National Institute of standards and technology (NIST) defines cloud computing as follows:

"Cloud computing is a model for enabling convenient, on-demand network access to a shared pool of configurable computing resources (e.g., networks, servers, storage, applications, and services) that can be rapidly provisioned and released with minimal management effort or service provider interaction."

In simpler terms, the cloud can be described as a service provider or vendor who delivers everything from computing power to infrastructure, storage to applications, business processes etc as a service wherever and whenever we need.

Therefore, cloud computing is purely a service and not an architecture. The cloud services are available in various types.

The major classifications are:

- Service models: Cloud models are explained in terms of the type of services they offer.
- Deployment models: Here the various cloud models are differentiated in terms of availability they offer to the customers.

The other types can also be described in terms of architecture, virtualization, etc.

Software as a Service (SaaS)
Software-as-a-Service provides complete applications to a cloud's end user. This can be mainly accessed through a web portal and service oriented architectures based on web service technologies. Instead of obtaining desktop and server licenses for software products it uses, an enterprise can obtain the same functions through a hosted service from a provider through a network connection. The interface to the software is usually through a web browser. This common cloud-computing model is known as Software as a Service (SaaS) or a hosted software model and the provider is known as the SaaS Provider. SaaS saves the complexity of software installation, maintenance, upgrades since the software is managed centrally at the SaaS provider's facilities.

Platform as a Service
Platform as a Service (PaaS) provides a software platform on which users can build their own applications and host them on the provider's infrastructure. PaaS provides basic software platform or framework for its client on which he can build their software application effectively. Here the client/cloud user does not need to worry about the scalability of the underlying platform and can focus on his development.

Infrastructure as a Service (IaaS)
Infrastructure as a service or IaaS offers you the greatest degree of control of the three models. In this model provider offers various "raw" computing provisions, storage and network infrastructure where you can load your own software. In IaaS, scaling and elasticity is the customer's responsibility. This scenario is like a hosting provider provisioning physical web servers and storage and makes you install your own operating system and other software to this infrastructure.

Deployment Models
The various deployment models as identified by NIST can be given as follows.

- Public cloud: The cloud infrastructure is made available to the general public and is controlled and owned by a cloud service provider.
- Private cloud: The cloud infrastructure is operated solely for the organization.
There are two cloud types:
    - Onsite private cloud: Private cloud implemented at customer's premises.
    - Outsourced private cloud: Private cloud where the server side is outsourced to a hosting vendor.
- Community cloud: In a community cloud, the infrastructure is shared by several firms that have a similar set of concerns in terms of security requirements, policies, target audience, etc. Community cloud can have two possible types, as in the case of private clouds.
    - Onsite community cloud
    - Outsourced community cloud
- Hybrid cloud: Cloud infrastructure where the composition consists of two or more clouds which binds in such a way that it does not lose its individuality are called hybrid cloud.

 Security in a Cloud

Cloud computing is a model for information and services by using existing technologies. It uses the internet infrastructure to allow communication between client side and server side services/applications. Cloud service providers (CSP's) exist between clients that offers cloud platforms for their customers to use and create their own web services. When making decisions to adopt cloud services, privacy or security has always been a major issue. To deal with these issues, the cloud provider must build up sufficient controls to provide such level of security than the organization would have if the cloud were not used.

The top seven security issues as described by NIST are

- Abuse and nefarious use of cloud computing
- Insecure interfaces and APIs
- Malicious insiders
- Shared technology issues
- Data loss or leakage
- Account or service hijacking
- Unknown risk profile

Multi tenancy and virtualization are important issues in cloud computing.
- Some of the risks that are associated with multi tenancy can be reduced with data segregation.
- Software and services that are not necessary for the implementation should be removed or should be disabled.
- The firmware updates and the software /OS patches should be kept current, and the audit log files should be carefully monitored.
- The vulnerabilities in the implementation of the system should be found before others (hackers) do and work with your service provider to close these holes.
- Data storage on the cloud, can be made secure by using strong encryption methods or introducing VPN routing and forwarding.
- Backups should be performed regularly should be encrypted and stored in safe locations with high priority for access control.

Virtual Private Networks

Virtual private network is a point to point communication tunnel over an intermediary non-trusted network, mostly internet. Proper authentication methods and strong encryption methods are used for protecting the encapsulated traffic. Encryption is not necessary for the connection to be considered as a VPN. Most commonly, VPN is associated with the establishment of secure communication paths through the internet between two distant networks. VPN can either connect two individual systems or two networks. VPNs can also link routers firewalls switches and servers.

The main reason of having a VPN is to provide security for various legacy application that rely mostly on vulnerable methodologies or protocols. A VPN link can be established over any other network communication connection such as a simple wired LAN, or a WLAN or even for accessing an office LAN using an internet connection. VPN connects two distant network and make them work like a single network. The implementation of VPN can be done using software or hardware solutions. There are four common VPN protocols which are PPTP, L2F, L2TP and IPSec.

PPTP, L2F and L2TP operate at the data link layer of the OSI model. Server socket layer (SSL) can also be used as a VPN protocol which is most commonly used as session encryption tool used on the top of TCP. Point to point tunneling protocol is basically is developed from the point to point protocol (PPP).This tunneling protocol (PPTP) not only creates a tunnel across the untrusted network between the two systems but also encapsulates the data packets. Various authentication protocols are used for this purpose for giving proper protection to the data that is been communicated. The various authentication algorithms includes

- Microsoft Challenge Handshake Authentication Protocol (MS - CHAP)
- Challenge Handshake Authentication Protocol (CHAP)
- Password Authentication Protocol (PAP)
- Extensible Authentication Protocol (EAP)

There are also other VPN protocols other than PPTP, which adds more functionality to the protocol like better traffic encryption standards and better authentication methods, etc. L2TP uses IPSec to provide traffic encryption. In the same way, Cisco developed L2F which have a mutual authentication scheme. IP sec is the most commonly used and stable VPN protocol since it provides encryption and most secured authentication. IP sec protocol have two basic components or functions.

- Authenticating head: provides authentication.
- Encapsulating payload: provides encryption.

IP sec operates on network layer and can be used either in a tunnel mode or on a transport mode.

The main difference between these two modes is that the transport mode provides encryption to the IP packet data but not to the header of the packet. In tunnel mode, the entire IP packet along with the header is encrypted and a new header is added to the packet.

Virtual Machines

Virtualization can be thought of as a key component of cloud computing. Virtualization is made possible by abstracting the hardware and making it available to the virtual machines. This abstraction is usually done using a hypervisor. Hypervisor can be of two types. Type I (bare metal) or Type II (hosted). The Type I hypervisor model, also known as bare metal, is independent of the operating system and boots before the OS. The Type II hypervisor model, also known as hosted, is dependent on the operating system and cannot boot until the OS is up and running. It needs the OS to stay up so that it can boot.

In a cloud, the machine on which virtualization software is running is known as a host whereas the virtual machines are known as guests. A virtual machine (VM) can be described as a software implementation of a machine which processes and executes various applications like a normal computer or machine. Virtual machines, according to their degree of correspondence or communication to the real machine and their use can be categorized into two classes:

A system virtual machine provides a complete which supports the execution of a complete operating system (OS). They are built with the purpose of either providing a platform to run programs where the real hardware is not available.

A process virtual machine is designed to run only one program, which means that it supports a single process. Such virtual machines are usually closely suited to one or more programming languages and built with the purpose of providing program portability and flexibility.

An essential characteristic of a virtual machine is that the software running inside is limited to the resources and abstractions provided by the virtual machine - it cannot break out of its virtual environment. The product VMWare creates individual virtual machines so that a user can run multiple operating systems on one computer at the same time. The JavaVirtual Machine (JVM), used by basically every web browser today, creates virtual machines (called sandboxes) in which Java applets run. This is a protection mechanism, because the sandbox contains the applet and does not allow it to interact with the operating system and file system directly. The activities that the applet attempts to carry out are screened by the JVM to see if they are safe requests. If the JVM determines that an activity is safe, then the JVM carries out the request on behalf of the applet.

Cloud, making use of a shared infrastructure and by proper cloud virtualization resides the users applications on virtual machines. These VMs are virtualized by some physical hardware and is managed by using hypervisor as described earlier. Hypervisor is responsible to allocate virtual memory and CPU scheduling to the various VMs. In order to ensure security, VMs that are been used by different tenants are separated or isolated from each other. Usually hypervisors are been targeted by hackers. Strong isolation should be employed to ensure that VMs are not able to impact or access the operations of other users running under the same cloud service provider.

The various vulnerabilities that should be considered, and handled while a organization is ready to move its application as well as data in to cloud are

Session Riding and Hijacking
Session hijacking refers to use of a valid session key to gain unauthorized access for the information or services residing on a computer system. It also refers to theft of a cookie used to authenticate a user to a remote server. Session riding refers to the hackers sending commands to a web application on behalf of the targeted user by just sending that user an email or tricking the user into visiting a specially crafted website. Session riding deletes user data, executes online transactions like bids or orders, sends spam to an intranet system via internet and changes system as well as network configurations or even opens the firewall.

Virtual Machine Escape
The ability for an attacker or malware to remotely exploit vulnerabilities in these systems and applications by capturing the VMs is a significant threat to virtualized cloud computing environments. Also, co-location of multiple VMs increases the intensity of the attacks. VM escape is a vulnerability that enables a guest-level VM to attack its host. In this type of vulnerability, the attacker runs code on a VM that eventually allows an OS running within it to break out and interact directly with the hypervisor It allows the attacker to access the host OS and all other VMs running on that particular host.

Insecure Cryptography
The hackers can decode any cryptographic mechanism or algorithm. It is very common to find flaws in cryptographic algorithm implementations, which can make any strong encryption fail.

There are some common measures of security that are applied to the various security threats experienced in the cloud. Snapshots take an image of a system at a particular point in time and preserves it. In most of the VM implementations we can take as many snapshots as you can. These contains a copy of the virtual machine settings, information on all virtual disks attached, and the memory state of the machine at the time of the snapshot. These can also be used for virtual machine cloning, allowing the machine to be copied for testing. Sandboxing involves running apps in restricted memory areas. By doing so, it is possible to limit the possibility of an app's crash, allowing a user to access another app or the data associated with it. Without sandboxing, the possibility exists that a crash in another customer's implementation.

NETWORK SECURITY

Network Security Protocols

Network security protocols are used to protect computer data in storage and the data in transit. The primary function that is used to protect information as it is communicated across a network is cryptography. Cryptography basically uses algorithms to encrypt data and make it scrambled so that it cannot be readable by unauthorized users. Generally, cryptography works with a set of procedures or protocols that manage the exchange of data between devices and networks. Together, these cryptographic protocols enhance secure data transfer.

Secure communication is very necessary since attackers try to eavesdrop on communications, modify messages in transit, and hijack exchanges between systems. Some of the tasks networks security protocols are commonly used to protect are file transfers, web communication, and virtual private networks (VPN).

File transfer protocol (FTP) is a common protocol used for transferring files across the network. The main problem with FTP is that the files sent are not encrypted and hence are able to be compromised. FTP servers can be sniffed using a packet sniffer and the website's IP address can intercept all communications between the webmaster and the site's server.

Secure file transfer protocol (SFTP) offers a more secure way to transfer files. SFTP is usually built upon secure shell (SSH) and is able to encrypt commands and data transfers over a network, thereby reducing the likelihood of interception attacks. The SSH cryptographic protocol is also resilient to impersonation attacks because the client and server are authenticated using digital certificates.

Secure sockets layer/transport layer security (SSL/TLS) can be used as the underlying protocol for SFTP.

Like SSH, SSL/TLS authenticates the identity of both the server and the client, as well as encrypts communications between the two. In addition to securing SFTP file transfers, SSL/TLS is used for securing e-mail communication. SSL is also used in conjunction with hypertext transfer protocol (HTTP) to encrypt communications between a browser and a web server in the form of HTTP over secure sockets layer (HTTPS). HTTPS encrypts communications and verifies the identity of a web server.

When performing private transactions over the internet, such as online banking, it generally is good practice for a person to check the browser's address bar to make sure that the website's address begins with https:// and not just http://.

Another area where cryptographic network security protocols play an important role, especially for modern businesses, is in exchanging documents between private networks over a public internet connection. These so-called virtual private networks (VPNs) are critical for business because they securely connect remote workers and offices across the world. Some commonly used network security protocols that are used to facilitate VPNs are point-to-point tunneling protocol (PPTP), layer 2 tunneling protocol (L2TP), IP security (IPsec), and SSH. Not only do these network security protocols create a safe connection but they also greatly reduce the costs associated with creating an alternate solution, such as building or leasing lines to create a private network.

 Ports

Ports are special addresses that allow communication between hosts. In simple terms, ports identify how a communication process occurs. A port number is added from the source, indicating which port to communicate with on a server. If a server has a port defined and available for use (open), it will send back a message accepting the request. If the port is not valid, or is closed the server will refuse the connection.

The Internet Assigned Numbers Authority (IANA) has defined a list of ports called well-known ports. A port address or number is nothing but a bit of additional information added either to the TCP or UDP message. This information is added in the header of the packet. The layer below it encapsulates the message with its header. On a security point of view some of these ports are more prone to hacker attacks.

- Port No:0 This is most commonly used to help to determine the operating system. This port is considered invalid and thus generates a different response from a closed port. This is one among those ports which is attacked and provides the attacker knowledge of the OS that is been used.
- Port No:7 This port is commonly used for running the service echo. Echo is an out dated service that echoes whatever is sent to it. This is often used in DoS attacks.
- Port No:11 The service that can be run is sysstat. This is a UNIX service that lists all the running processes on a machine and who started them. This also has a very high attack rate.
- Port No:19 The UDP version of this service responds with a packet containing garbage characters. Whenever a UDP packet is received, on a TCP connection, it displays a stream of garbage characters until the connection is closed. The probability of attack is high and this is often used in DoS attacks.
- Port No:21 Used in for FTP service (file transfer protocol). Attack rate is very high. Attackers look for open anonymous FTP servers, those with directories that can be written to and read from.
- Port No:69 The service tftp is run (trivial file transfer protocol) and the attack rate is very high.
- Port No:98 The service linuxconf is run. This provides administration of Linux servers.
- Port No:513 The service name is rwho. This provides remote login (rlogin). Attack rate is very high.
- Port No:1080 The service SOCKS runs here. This protocol tunnels traffic through firewalls, allowing many people behind the firewall to access the internet through a single IP address. The rate of hacker attacks is very high. Theoretically, this protocol should only tunnel inside traffic out toward the in-

ternet. However, it is frequently mis-configured and allows attackers to tunnel their attacks into the network.
- Port No:31337 The service back orifice runs here. Error rate is very high. This is a common port for installing trojans.

Network Scanning

Network scanning is a procedure for identifying active hosts in a network, either for the purpose of attacking them or for network security assessment. The various scanning techniques like ping sweeps and port scans, return information about which IP addresses map to live hosts that are active on the internet and what services they offer. Another scanning technique called inverse mapping, returns information about what IP addresses do not map to live hosts hence enabling an attacker to make assumptions about reachable addresses.

From a hacker's view point, network scanning is one of three steps of information gathering for an impending attack. The attack always has three phases:

Foot printing phase creates the profile of the target organization, with the basic information such as its domain name system (DNS) and e-mail servers, and its IP address range.

Scanning phase finds information about the specific IP addresses from the range of IPs from the foot print stage that can be accessed over the internet. The attacker also manages to gather information about operating systems, the system architecture, and the services running on each computer of the respective organization.

Enumeration phase includes information such as network user and group names, routing tables, and simple network management protocol (SNMP) data is gathered in this stage

Network Management Analysis

Network management and analysis can be defined as a function that initializes, monitors, tests, configures, modifies and trouble shoots the operations of network components so that the entire network meets the expectations of the organization. The major functions that are performed by a network management system can be divided into five modules or categories.

They are

- Configuration management: This management function keeps track of the status of the entities in the network and also the relation of it with the other entities. Configuration management have two sub systems: reconfiguration and documentation. Reconfiguration is basically adjusting the parameters of the network components according to the changing scenarios of the network. There are three types of reconfigurations that can occur. Hardware reconfiguration that covers all the changes of the hardware. Software reconfiguration that covers all the changes that can occur in a software. User-account configuration adds and deletes users on a system. Documentation records all the hardware, software and user account configuration.

- Fault management: An area of network management that handles the proper operation of each component individually and with each other. Every effective fault management system has two subsystems: reactive fault management and proactive fault management. A reactive fault management system is responsible for detecting, isolating, correcting and recording faults where as proactive fault management system tries to prevent faults from occurring.

- Performance management: This is closely related to fault management and ensures that the network is running smoothly and efficiently. This also quantifies the performance by using some measurable items like capacity, throughput, traffic and response time.

- Security management: This is responsible for controlling access to the network based on a predefined policy.

- Accounting management: The control of users access to network resources through charges.

The basic framework for managing the network components in an internet is provided by SNMP also known as simple network management protocol. This functions by using a TCP/IP suit. SNMP uses the concept of manager and agent where the manager is usually the host that controls and monitors a group of agents, usually routers. SNMP is an application level protocol. The management with SNMP is based on three basic principles.

- Manager checks agent by requesting information that eventually reflects the behavior of the agent.
- Manager forces an agent to perform a task by resetting values in the agent database.

- An agent contributes to the management process by warning the manager of an unusual situation.

SNMP uses structure of management information (SMI) and management information base (MIB) protocols more for the management of the components. The roles of these three protocols in performing the network management is as follows:

- SNMP defines the format of the packets exchanged between the manager and an agent. It also reads and changes the status values of objects in SNMP packets.
- SMI defines the general rules for naming objects, defining object types and also showing how to encode objects and values.
- MIB creates a collection of named objects, their types and their relationship with each other in an entity to be managed.

Cryptography

Cryptography is a method of protecting information by scrambling it so that even if the intruders get access to the data they cannot read it. Cryptography is the science of transforming the confidential data into a more secure form so that it can be transmitted through a public channel or can be stored without the fear of unauthorized access. There are more methods and applications of cryptography.

Steganography is another method of message hiding, in which the message or the data that should be kept secure is hidden inside an image. This data then can be decoded using some effective algorithms at the receiving end. One of the most famous ancient cryptographers was Julius Caesar. In messages to his commanders, Caesar shifted each letter of his messages three places down in the alphabet, so that an A was replaced by a D, a B was replaced by an E, and so forth. The generalized form is known as a substitution cipher.

Cryptography can provide basic security protection for information.

- Cryptography can protect the confidentiality of information by ensuring that only authorized parties can view it.
- Cryptography can protect the integrity of the information. Integrity ensures that the information is correct and no unauthorized person or malicious software has altered that data.
- Cryptography can help ensure the availability of the data so that authorized users (with the key) can access it.

Hash Algorithms

The most basic type of cryptographic algorithm is a hash algorithm. Hashing is a process for creating a unique digital fingerprint for a set of data. This fingerprint, called a hash (sometimes called a one-way hash or digest) represents the contents. Although hashing is considered a cryptographic algorithm, its purpose is not to create a cipher text that can later be decrypted.

Instead, hashing is "one-way" in that its contents cannot be used to reveal the original set of data. Hashing is primarily used for comparison purposes. A practical example of a hash algorithm is used with some automated teller machine (ATM) cards. A bank customer has a personal identification number (PIN) of 93542. This number is hashed and the result is permanently stored on a magnetic stripe on the back of the ATM card. When visiting an ATM, the customer is asked to insert the card and then enter a PIN on a keypad. The ATM takes the PIN entered and hashes it with the same algorithm used to create the hash stored on the card. If the two values match, then the user can access the ATM.

A variation that provides improved security is the hashed message authentication code (HMAC). HMAC begins with a shared secret key that is in the possession of both the sender and receiver. The sender creates a hash and then encrypts that hash with the key before transmitting it with the original data. The receiver uses their key to decrypt the hash and then creates their own hash of the data, comparing the two values.

Message Digest

One common hash algorithm is the Message digest (MD) algorithm, which has three versions. Message digest 2 (MD2) takes plaintext of any length and creates a hash 128 bits long. MD2 begins by dividing the message into 128-bit sections. If the message is fewer than 128 bits, data known as padding is added. Message digest 4 (MD4) was developed in 1990 for computers that processed 32 bits at a time. Like MD2, MD4 takes plaintext and creates a hash of 128 bits. The plaintext message itself is padded to a length of 512 bits instead of 128 bits as with MD2. Flaws in the MD4 hash algorithm have prevented this MD from being widely accepted. Message digest 5 (MD5), a revision of MD4, was created the following year and designed to address MD4's weaknesses. Like MD4, the length of a message is padded to 512 bits. The hash algorithm then uses four variables of 32 bits each in a round-robin fashion to create a value that is compressed to generate the hash.

Secure Hash Algorithm (SHA)

A more secure hash than MD is the secure hash algorithm (SHA). Like MD, the SHA is a family of hashes. The first version was SHA-0, yet due to a flaw it was withdrawn shortly after it was first released. It successor, SHA-1, is patterned after MD4 and MD5, but creates a hash that is 160 bits in length instead of 128 bits. SHA pads messages of fewer than 512 bits with zeros and an integer that describes the original length of the message. The padded message is then run through the SHA algorithm to produce the hash.

Whirlpool
Whirlpool is a relatively recent cryptographic hash function that has received international recognition and adoption by standards organizations, including the International Organization for Standardization (ISO). Named after the first galaxy recognized to have a spiral structure, it creates a hash of 512 bits. Whirlpool is being implemented in several new commercial cryptography applications.

RACE Integrity Primitives Evaluation Message Digest (RIPEMD)
Another hash was developed by the research and development in Advanced Communications Technologies (RACE) organization, which is affiliated with the European Union (EU). RIPEMD stands for RACE Integrity Primitives Evaluation Message Digest, which was designed after MD4.

Password Hashes
Another use for hashes is in storing passwords. When a password for an account is created, the password is hashed and stored. When a user enters her password to log in, that password is likewise hashed and compared with the stored hashed version; if the two hashes match, then the user is authenticated.

Symmetric Algorithms
Symmetric cryptographic algorithms use the same shared single key to encrypt and decrypt a document. Unlike hashing in which the hash is not intended to be decrypted, symmetric algorithms are designed to encrypt and decrypt the ciphertext; a document encrypted with a symmetric cryptographic algorithm by Nick will be decrypted when received by Stacy. It is therefore essential that the key be kept confidential, because if an attacker obtained the key, he could read all the encrypted documents. For this reason, symmetric encryption is also called private key cryptography.

Data Encryption Standard (DES)
One of the first widely popular symmetric cryptography algorithms was the data encryption standard (DES). DES is a block cipher. It divides plaintext into 64-bit blocks and then executes the algorithm 16 times. There are four modes of DES encryption. Although DES was once widely implemented, its 56-bit key is no longer considered secure and has been broken several times. It is not recommended for use.

Advanced Encryption Standard (AES)
The advanced encryption standard (AES) is a symmetric cipher that was approved by NIST in late 2000 as a replacement for DES. AES performs three steps on every block (128 bits) of plaintext. Within step 2, multiple rounds are performed depending on the key size: a 128-bit key performs 9 rounds, a 192-bit key performs 11 rounds, and a 256-

bit key, known as AES-256, uses 13 rounds. Within each round, bytes are substituted and rearranged, and then special multiplication is performed based on the new arrangement. AES is designed to be secure well into the future.

Triple Data Encryption Standard (3DES)

Triple Data Encryption Standard (3DES) is designed to replace DES. As its name implies, 3DES uses three rounds of encryption instead of just one. The ciphertext of one round becomes the entire input for the second iteration. 3DES employs a total of 48 iterations in its encryption (3 iterations times 16 rounds).

Asymmetric Cryptographic Algorithms

A completely different approach from symmetric cryptography is asymmetric cryptographic algorithms, also known as public key cryptography. Asymmetric encryption uses two keys instead of only one. These keys are mathematically related and are known as the public key and the private key. The public key is known to everyone and can be freely distributed, while the private key is known only to the individual to whom it belongs.

There are several important principles regarding asymmetric cryptography:

- Key pairs. Unlike symmetric cryptography that uses only one key, asymmetric cryptography requires a pair of keys.
- Public key. Public keys by their nature are designed to be "public" and do not need to be protected. They can be freely given to anyone or even posted on the internet.
- Private key. The private key should be kept confidential and never shared.
- Both directions. Asymmetric cryptography keys can work in both directions. A document encrypted with a public key can be decrypted with the corresponding private key. In the same way, a document encrypted with a private key can be decrypted with its public key.

The RSA algorithm multiplies two large prime numbers (a prime number is a number divisible only by itself and 1), p and q, to compute their product (n = pq). Next, a number e is chosen that is less than n and a prime factor to (p-1)(q-1). Another number d is determined, so that (ed-1) is divisible by (p-1)(q-1). The values of e and d are the public and private exponents. The public key is the pair (n,e), while the private key is (n,d). The numbers p and q can be discarded.

Elliptic Curve Cryptography (ECC)

Elliptic curve cryptography (ECC) was first proposed in the mid-1980s. Instead of using large prime numbers as with RSA, elliptic curve cryptography uses sloping curves. An elliptic curve is a function drawn on an X-Y axis as a gently curved line. By adding the values of two points on the curve, a third point on the curve can be derived.

With ECC, users share one elliptic curve and one point on the curve. One user chooses a secret random number and computes a public key based on a point on the curve; the other user does the same. They can now exchange messages because the shared public keys can generate a private key on an elliptic curve.

Quantum Cryptography

Quantum cryptography attempts to use the unusual and unique behavior of microscopic objects to enable users to securely develop and share keys as well as to detect eavesdropping Quantum cryptography exploits the properties of microscopic objects such as photons. A possible scenario for quantum cryptography is as follows:

- Using a special device, Stacy observes photons randomly that have specific circular, diagonal, or other types of polarizations. She records the polarization of each photon and then sends it to Nick.
- When Nick receives each photon, he randomly measures its polarization and records it.
- Nick then tells Stacy publicly what his measurements types were, but not the results of the measurements.
- Stacy responds back telling Nick which measurement types were correct. Stacy and Nick then convert the correct types to a string of bits that forms their secret key.

If quantum cryptography is found to be commercially feasible, it may hold the potential for introducing an entirely new type of cryptography.

NTRUEncrypt

A newer asymmetric cryptographic algorithm is NTRUEncrypt. NTRUEncrypt uses a unique foundation, rather than prime numbers (RSA) or points on a curve (ECC). Instead, it uses lattice-based cryptography that relies on a set of points in space. In addition to being faster than RSA and ECC, it is believed the NTRUEncrypt will be more resistant to quantum computing attacks.

WEP/WPA/WPA2

Wireless systems, are systems that don't use wires to send information but rather transmit data through the air.

Wired equivalent privacy (WEP) was intended to provide basic security for wireless networks, but now wireless systems frequently use the wireless application protocol (WAP) as a security measure for wireless network communications. WPA and WPA2 have replaced WEP in most implementations.

Wired equivalent privacy (WEP) is a wireless protocol designed to provide a privacy equivalent to that of a wired network. WEP was vulnerable because of weaknesses in the way its encryption algorithms (RC4) are employed. These weaknesses allowed the algorithm to be cracked potentially in as little as five minutes using available PC software. This made WEP one of the more vulnerable security protocols. To strengthen WEP encryption, a temporal key integrity protocol (TKIP) was employed. This placed a 128-bit wrapper around the WEP encryption with a key that is based on things such as the MAC address of the destination device and the serial number of the packet. TKIP was designed as a backward-compatible replacement to WEP, and it could work with all existing hardware.

Wireless application protocol (WAP) is a technology designed for use with wireless devices. WAP functions are equivalent to TCP/IP functions in that they're attempting to serve the same purpose for wireless devices. WAP uses a smaller version of HTML called wireless markup language (WML).

WAP-enabled devices can also respond to scripts using an environment called WMLScript. The ability to accept web pages and scripts allows malicious code and viruses to be transported to WAP-enabled devices. WAP systems communicate using a WAP gateway system. The gateway converts information back and forth between HTTP and WAP as well as encodes and decodes between the protocols.

If the interconnection between the WAP server and the internet isn't encrypted, packets between the devices may be intercepted, referred to as packet sniffing, creating a potential vulnerability. This vulnerability is called a gap in the WAP, i.e., the security concern that exists when converting between WAP and SSL/TLS and exposing plain text.

There are several levels of security exist in WAP: anonymous authentication allows virtually anyone to connect to the wireless portal. Server authentication requires the workstation to authenticate against the server. Two-way (client and server) authentication requires both ends of the connection (client and server) to authenticate to confirm validity.

If wireless APs are installed in a building, the signals will frequently radiate past the inside of the building, and they can be detected and decoded outside the building using inexpensive equipment. The term war driving refers to driving around town with a laptop looking for APs to communicate with. The network card on the intruder's laptop is set to promiscuous mode, and it looks for signals coming from anywhere. After intruders gain access, they may steal internet access or corrupt your data. Once weaknesses have been discovered in a wireless network, war chalking can occur. War chalking involves those who discover a way into the network leaving signals (often written in chalk) on, or outside, the premise to notify others that a vulnerability exists there.

The difference between WPA and WPA2 is that, WPA uses the RC4 encryption algorithm with TKIP, whereas WPA2 implements the full standard and is not compatible with older devices. Although WPA mandates the use of TKIP, WPA2 requires counter mode with cipher block chaining message authentication code protocol (CCMP). CCMP uses 128-bit AES encryption with a 48-bit initialization vector. The larger initialization vector in WPA2, increases the difficulty in cracking and minimizes the risk of a replay attack.

WEP/WPA cracking
A wireless network that is protected by WEP is not considered secure in modern times. The attacker only has to has to determine the WEP key, and is merely a task of seconds. Once the attacker has determined the key, he can get inside your system and monitor traffic or even take on the role of administrator and change the settings. WPA uses a security mechanism called temporal key integrity protocol (TKIP). But this is not also very secure, and is prone to fail and get decrypted to certain hacker attacks. The muck better option is to use WPA2 that uses an AES.

Firewall/IDS/IPS

A firewall is a device installed between the internal network of an organization and the rest of the internet. The basic design of any firewall allows forwarding of some packets and filtration of some. This can be used to deny access to some host or a specific service in the organization.

Firewalls have two categories:

- Packet filter firewall
- Proxy based firewall

A packet filter firewall is a special type of router that uses a filtering table to determine which packets to be discarded. The user can feed in all those source IP, destination IP and port numbers in order to filter those packets which either originate or destined to those IPS or ports.

A proxy firewall is able to open an incoming packet at the application level and find out whether that packet is legitimate or not. If the packet is legitimate, then the firewall sends the message to the real server or else that packet is dropped.

The main difference between these two types of firewalls is that while the packet filter firewall filters at the network/transport layer proxy firewall filters at the application layer.

IDS vs. IPS

Intrusion detection system
Any activity of an intruder to penetrate into a network can be detected by analyzing the data packets communicated through the network. Here both the headers and the payloads are analyzed. This technique is known as intrusion detection. Currently, there are hardware devices as well as software applications used for this purpose. They are generally known as intrusion detection systems. These systems generate log messages whenever an intrusion is detected. These messages can be given as alerts to the network administrator. Intrusion detection systems can also be found as an add-on feature on a normal firewall. The advantage of an IDS is that it can intelligently monitor and differentiate between a normal traffic scenario and a traffic with intrusion. Also, most of the IDS comes with the latest attack signatures vendor itself.

Intrusion Prevention System is defined as a device or an application that analyzes whole packets, both header and payload, looking for known events. When a known event is detected then the packet is rejected.

The main difference between an intrusion prevention system (IPS) and IDS is that the IPS can take more action in response to a threat. An IPS can address an identified threat by resetting a connection or even closing a port. IPS can also be configured so that it can alert the administrator about the threat and the action that was taken by the system. The types of IDS and IPS can be categorized on the basis of the underlying methods used.

Behavior based
The IDS/IPS is generally software that is installed on the host to monitor the data packets and detect and potentially respond to anything or anyone attempting to breach the security policy. It can dynamically inspect network packets and determine which programs use which resources during a normal working day. Hence it learns what exactly is meant by a normal data packet and it can detect an event that is not normal and alert the administrator to take action by closing ports and connections.

Signature based
A signature-based IDS/IPS starts off with a database of known attacks and is capable of recognizing those attacks. The only negative point is that if the attack that is occurring is not in the database of signatures, then it won't be recognized by a purely signature-based IDS/IPS.

Network based
A network-based appliance is generally located on the edge of a network where that network comes in contact with another network such as the internet.

Host based
These are software based firewalls that are used to control traffic to a single host. They are referred to as host based system. The Windows Firewall on Microsoft Windows operating systems is a prime example of a firewall that comes with the operating system.

Next generation firewall
This enforces a pre programmed security policy unilaterally across more than just network packet header information. This can make a single device act as both a traditional firewall and IPS.

PHYSICAL & ENVIRONMENTAL SECURITY

Physical Security

The term physical and environmental security refers to different security measures taken to protect systems, buildings, and related supporting infrastructure of information assets against threats associated with their physical environment.

Physical and environmental security controls include the following three broad areas:

1. The physical facility is usually the building, other structure, or vehicle housing the system and network components.
2. The facility's general geographic operating location determines the characteristics of natural threats, which include earthquakes and flooding. Man-made threats such as burglary, civil disorders are also included here.
3. Supporting facilities are those services (both technical and human) that are essential for the healthy operation of the system. These are facilities such as electric power, heating and air conditioning, and telecommunications. The failure of these facilities may interrupt operation of the system and may cause physical damage to system hardware or stored data.

Physical Access Management
Physical access management deals with managing the various strategies that can be used to physically control and monitor the access to the computers other related equipments. Physical access control can be broadly be classified into two types

- Preventive physical controls
- Detective physical controls

Preventive physical controls prevent unauthorized personnel from entering to the highly vulnerable areas like the server room, data processing facilities and other important areas. Some of the preventive physical controls include:

- Backing up data files
- Erecting fences to protect the building from intruders
- Appointing security guards
- Having a identity smart card system
- Biometric access control systems
- Electronic locks
- Double door systems

Detective physical controls give away warning signals when the security measures are violated or breached. Some of these controls include

- Motion detectors
- Fire and smoke detectors
- CCTV monitors

Biometrics

Biometric systems are those access control systems which uses some biological trait to identify a person. The various biometric access controls includes: finger print scanners which users a person's finger print to give the access, retinal scanners that matches patterns in human retina, facial recognition applications and also key stroke recognition programs. Usually these are paired with other security systems that monitor and record all authorized and unauthorized access attempts.

As described earlier, biometric systems identifies a person by measuring a particular biological trait and then compares it with a library of characteristics belonging to various other people. Hence, biometric access control systems are basically a pattern recognition system. The basic working of a biometric system can be explained as follows:

- The biometric sensor takes an observation depending up on its type. This is known as the biometric signature of that person.
- The biometric signature is then normalized by a computer algorithm so as to make it similar to the same format as the other signatures in the database.

- The matcher then compares this signature with the other signatures that are already stored in the system database.

The above three step procedure is done by using the four components of any biometric system.

- Sensor module: helps in taking the observation.
- Feature extraction module: extracts feature values of the biological trait.
- Matching module: matches with the database.
- Decision making module: takes decision whether to give access or not.

FAR/FRR/FER/Crossover Error Rates

False acceptance rate (FAR) is the probability when a biometric system incorrectly identifies an individual or incorrectly verifies an intruder with a non matching pattern against a claimed identity. This is measured by taking the percentage of invalid matches. This is also known as false match rate (FMR) or type II error.

This is calculated as follows:

FAR = NFA / NIIA or FAR = NFA / NIVA
FAR is the false acceptance rate
NFA is the number of false acceptances
NIIA is the number of impostor identification attempts
NIVA is the number of impostor verification attempts

False reject rate (FRR) is the probability that a biometric system will fail to identify a person enrolled or the pattern stored in the database, or verify the legitimate claimed identity of the person enrolled. This is measured as the percent of valid inputs that is being rejected. This is also known as false non-match rate (FNMR) or type I error.

This is measured as follows:
FRR = NFR / NEIA or FRR = NFR / NEVA
FRR is the false rejection rate
NFR is the number of false rejections
NEIA is the number of input pattern identification attempts
NEVA is the number of input pattern verification attempts

Failure to enroll rate (FTE or FER): The percentage of data input is considered invalid and fails to input into the system. Failure to enroll happens when the data obtained by the sensor are considered invalid or of poor quality.

Crossover Error Rate (CER) represents the point at which the false reject rate equals the false acceptance rate. It is good for comparing different biometric systems. A system with a CER of 3 will be more accurate than a system with a CER of 4.

 Media Management

Media management refers to the various steps that should be taken care of in order to protect media and the data it contains. Here, in this context, media is anything that can hold data. Tapes, CD, DVDs, Portable USBs, both internal and external hard disk (SATA) drives, USB flash drives are all examples of media. Also, the various portable devices such as tables and smart phones include memory cards that can hold data can be grouped as media.

Specially tapes are used commonly for taking data backups and thus contains sensitive data. The management of these media is very crucial. The main points that should be taken care of while managing data are:

- Location, where the media is stored. The location should be secure with strict access controls that prohibits unauthorized entry.
- Temperature and humidity. Proper temperature/humidity controls should be installed to prevent losses to corruption.
- Various technical controls. If a particular media connected to the system is detected as having a virus, there should be proper controls to detect and disable that.

Another important aspect that to be discussed is media disposal.

Media disposal deals with the various aspects of disposal of the different types of media and how the data contained is removed for recycle and when this is allowed. NIST mainly discusses the different methods for this as media sanitation methods. The commonly used media sanitation methods are:

Disposal: This method is nothing but throwing away or discarding any media including CDs, DVDs, etc., without any direct or indirect media sanitization method.

Cleaning: Another media sanitization method which is more concentrated on protecting the confidentiality and privacy of information recorded in the media is known as cleaning. In cleaning, the main aim is on the protection of information against different types of keyboard attacks. This method includes simple removal of items by deletions as well as ensuring that the information (once removed) is not retrieved back using any sort of data or file recovery techniques or procedures.

Purging: This is stronger type of media sanitization technique where the information destroyed from a media cannot be retrieved using any lab based data retrieval methods. Lab based data retrieval methods involves physical removal of the storage media and usage of sophisticated retrieval techniques both hardware and software in an off-site lab environment. One of the major purging methods that are used are the execution of the firmware secure erase command. Degaussing is another purging method that is been widely used.

Degaussing is a method used to clean a magnetic field on an existing device or media. The method was used by war ships to clean any residual magnetic field created by the vessel while travelling to wipe off magnetic signatures to prevent destruction from mines. The apparatus used was known as a degausser. Degaussing is also used to clean or wipe data off a magnetic media by exposing to a small field called a bias.

Destroying: Destruction of media is the most permanent form of sanitization. After media is destroyed, they cannot be reused as originally intended. Some other methods of destruction of media are disintegration, incineration, pulverization, and melting. These sanitization methods are designed to completely destroy the media.

Shredding: shredders are used to destroy flexible media like diskettes, CDs and paper materials.

Environmental Controls

The location of IT resources in an organization is crucial for its security and privacy. Hackers and intruders can utilize this for getting access to the organization's sensitive information assets. Environment controls can be explained as those elements of environment like temperature or humidity which directly or indirectly controls the overall health of the computer systems. The various environment controls can be categorized into HVAC controls, fire suppression controls, EMI shielding, hot and cold aisles, environmental monitoring, temperature and humidity controls.

HVAC controls: HVAC, the heating, ventilation and air conditioning needs of any asset which is a part of information system of an organization falls in this category.

Fire suppression controls: Fire suppression is a very important environment security element in organizations because fires can cause complete destruction to the computer hardware and data and even precious human lives. Prevention techniques can be exercised depending upon the factors that can cause fire.

EMI shielding: Shielding is a process of armoring computer systems to prevent an intelligent intruder to decode information from the electronic emissions from the system. Shielding also prevents unwanted electronic emissions or signals from outside to eavesdrop or disturb the system. A faraday cage is an example used for shielding. In this method, a electrically conductor mesh is woven into a box which can cover the computer room is used.

Hot and cold aisles: The cooling systems used to prevent overheating in server racks are known as hot and cold aisles. The rows of servers in a server are cooled with hot aisles by introducing hot air outlets whereby cold aisles introduces cool air intake for cooling the equipment.

Environmental monitoring: The various concerns like flood, fire, water, smoke can cause mass destruction of the entire data center itself. Proper prevention and detection methods should be installed in order to avoid the issues that can be caused by these factors. Continuous monitoring procedures should be followed. Installation of smoke detectors triggering a fire alarm, and moisture detectors which triggers automatic power off of the computer room are very important.

Temperature and humidity controls: Large mainframe and supercomputers can produce a considerable amount of heat while processing. It is very important to monitor the temperature, since overheating or an increase in temperature can deteriorate the performance of servers or can even corrupt data. The humidity level should also be monitored since if it goes below 50%, there is a chance for the damage from electrostatic shock, hence this should be regulated using a proper monitoring and prevention system.

Tailgating: This is the method of getting entry to electronically locked rooms or buildings by following someone through the door they just unlocked.

Fail Safe vs. Fail Secure

Fail safe lock are those locks which will be locked when it is energized. These type of locks need power to lock. When the power is interrupted, this lock will disengage.

Fail secure lock also needs to be energized but when the lock system is energized this is unlocked.

VULNERABILITY MANAGEMENT

 ## *Testing the Network*

Hackers usually target those organizations, where the networks are poorly managed and unprotected. Thus the proper installation of an antivirus solution on all end points and other security measures like firewalls, etc., are of immense importance. Even though the network is protected with appropriate security measures, constant updating is needed since, these measures can get outdated in no time. This is why large companies usually hire penetration testers in order to keep a check on the health of their networks. Penetration tests constantly try to hack their own networks by ethical hacking tools. This will help them to discover the various vulnerabilities of their networks and also uncover any holes through which a real hacker can get an undue advantage on the network. The main problem with penetration testing is that, this is very expensive and also this will only reveal the state of the network at that particular point of time.

An alternative and less costly approach is to use software tools that scan your network and report on any vulnerabilities. The major software tools are listed below.

Port scans: This is used to identify any ports that are open on any given computer on your network.

Network scans: Scans all the components that are connected to your network and checks whether the network is secure or not.

Vulnerability scans: Unpatched or out of date applications are vulnerable to attacks. These scans provide this information. Some vulnerability scanners also find the SQL injection vulnerabilities of the web applications hosted in your server and also administrator accounts that are not password protected.

Rogue access point detection: Rouge access points are those wireless access points in the network that will not give the alert to the admin.

Automated penetration tests: Short of hiring a team of penetration testers, the most effective way to test for vulnerabilities on your network is to use automated penetration testing.

Bug bounty programs: As a low cost alternative to a penetration test, an increasing number of organizations offer to manage a bug bounty program on your behalf. Here these programs arrange for a large number of security researchers, former hackers and students to attempt to hack your system, paying rewards or bounties for any vulnerabilities that are found after they have checked and verified them.

Hacker Attacks

Hacker attacks are not automated by programs such as viruses, worms, or trojan horse programs. There are various forms that exploit weaknesses in security initiated by people or programmers. Many of these may cause loss of service or system crashes.
Spoofing: Spoofing is the action of making something look like something that it is not in order to gain unauthorized access to a user's private information. The idea of spoofing originated in the 1980s with the discovery of a security hole in the TCP protocol. The various forms of spoofing are IP, URL and email spoofing.

IP spoofing: IP spoofing is the act of manipulated the headers in a transmitted message to mask a hacker's true identity so that the message could appear as though it is from a trusted source. The hacker manipulates the packet by using tools to modify the source address field.

URL spoofing: URL spoofing occurs when one website appears as if it is another.

Email spoofing: Email spoofing is the act of altering the header of an email so that the email appears to be sent from someone else.

Smurfing: The attacks through internet Control Message Protocol (ICMP) messages, are known as a smurf attack. A smurf attack overflows network traffic which is a kind of denial of service attack where with the help of spoofed broadcast ping messages flooding of target system is done. Smurfing can make use of internet protocol (IP) and internet control message protocol (ICMP).

The various steps defining a smurf attack are:

- Victim IP address is to be identified by the attacker.
- Intermediary site is to be identified by attacker which helps in amplifying attack.
- Large amount of traffic will be sent by attacker to the broadcast address at particular intermediary sites.
- Intermediaries will provide broadcast to all hosts which are there in a subnet.
- Hosts will reply to network.

DoS and DDoS

DDoS: A denial of service (DoS) attack usually either involves attackers sending messages to exploit certain vulnerabilities leading to the abnormality of business systems, or sending a massive amount of regular messages quickly to a single node to run out the system resources resulting in business system failure. A distributed denial of service (DDoS) attack is a DoS attack utilizing multiple distributed attack sources.

How do DDoS attacks work?

Network packets use TCP/IP for transmission. The packets themselves are harmless, but if there are too many abnormal packets, it will cause the network devices or servers to overload. This can quickly consume the system resources. Another case is if the packets take advantage of certain protocol's defects (e.g. artificial incompleteness or malformation), causing the failure of network devices or servers. Both cases will result in denial of service. These are the basic principles of DDoS attacks.

In general, DDoS attacks can be divided into the following types:

Denial of service attack. DDoS or distributed denial of service, is a type of attack in which the legitimate user is denied of the service of the network to which he is entitled to.

Bandwidth-based attacks. This type of attack is one which sends unlimited junk data as messages causing an overload. This depletes the bandwidth of the network and reduces the resources of the equipments denying service of the network to the user.

Traffic based DDos attacks. In traffic based DDoS attacks, a large amount of TCP, UDP data packets which looks legitimate are flooded into a targeted system through the network. This make the network bandwidth towards that system becomes overloaded and hence network traffic becomes a stand still. These type of attack is also known as network flooding attacks.

Flooding attacks can be found in application level also.

Known as application based attacks, here the overloading is done by sending numerous application layer data messages. This causes overloading of certain system resources, hence making the targeted system's services unavailable.

DNS poisoning: DNS poisoning is a deliberate attempt to manipulate the system which converts domain names into its corresponding static IP addresses. Here by applying

DNS poisoning, the domain name is resolved into an incorrect IP address. This is done by changing the name records of a particular website. Thus whenever a user tries to access a particular site, either the site is shown unavailable or the user gets redirected to a different website.

Teardrops: Teardrops is a program which exploits the overlapping IP fragment bug present in operating systems such as Windows 95,Windows NT, etc. When two fragments inside a similar datagram overlaps on one on the other while trying to position itself in the datagram. The above operating systems fail to handle the situation and hence behave in a undesirable manner leading to loss of data and even crashing of the system. Teardrop attacks have a bot program which sends pieces of an illegitimate packet with some random data written on it. The operating system tries to reassemble fragments and eventually crashes.

Cross site scripting: Cross site scripting attack or CSS attack is a generic application level attack. CSS attacks are targeted towards the privacy of the various clients that visits a particular website. The modus operandi of CSS attack is stealing the client cookies, and other sensitive information of a particular website, including the identity and personal information of the various clients of that site. CSS attacks poses a challenge to the privacy of the various clients which visits the infected site.

Port scanning: This is a method where an attacker tries to find out which ports are open in a particular system by using a listening service. These ports which are accidently left open can be serious security threats.

Rootkits: Rootkits are malicious programs which controls the activities of a computer by successfully hiding its presence.

The name of these type of programs is originated from the traditional term "root" given to the administrator account of a Unix operating system. A rootkit program has an automated installation and allows a third-party to maintain the administrative control of the system without the knowledge of the owner of the system. It is very difficult to detect a rootkit program. No known antivirus or anti-malware products are available in the market, which can successfully trace, detect and remove rootkits. The various methods of detections includes behavioural based methods, signature scanning , difference scanning and so on. Removal of rootkits is very complex.

Various rootkits make their space inside the target systems by piggybacking with some software you download from the internet for installing or with some virus. One of the way to safeguard the system from rootkits by ensuring that the virus definitions and the various patches available for the OS and the applications are updated and is upgraded against known vulnerabilities.

In some cases where the rootkit is installed inside the kernel, the removal is practically impossible. In those cases formatting the drive and reinstalling the OS is the only available solution.

SQL injections: SQL (Structured Query Language) is used for communicating with online (and other relational) databases. With a SQL injection attack (also known as a SQL insertion attack), an attacker manipulates the database code to take advantage of a weakness in it. The way to defend against this attack is always to filter input. That means that the website code should check to see if certain characters are in the text fields and, if so, to reject that input.

Hoaxes: Hoax virus warnings or alerts have an odd double relation to viruses. First, hoaxes are usually warnings about new viruses, which new viruses that do not, of course, exist. Second, hoaxes generally carry a directive to the user to forward the warning to all addresses available to them. Thus, these descendants of chain letters form a kind of self-perpetuating spam. Many of the original hoax warnings stated only that you should not open a message with a certain phrase in the subject line.

Back door: The term backdoor attack can have two different meanings. The original term backdoor referred to troubleshooting and developer hooks into systems that often circumvented normal authentication. During the development of a complicated operating system or application, programmers add backdoors or maintenance hooks. Backdoors allow them to examine operations inside the code while the code is running. The backdoors are stripped out of the code when it's moved into production. When a software manufacturer discovers a hook that hasn't been removed, it releases a maintenance upgrade or patch to close the backdoor. These patches are common when a new product is initially released. The second type of backdoor refers to gaining access to a network and inserting a program or utility that creates an entrance for an attacker. The program may allow a certain user ID to log on without a password or to gain administrative privileges.

Brute force: A brute-force attack is an attempt to guess passwords until a successful guess occurs. Because of the nature of this routine, this type of attack usually occurs over a long period of time. To make passwords more difficult to guess, they should be much longer than two or three characters (six should be the bare minimum), be complex, and have password lockout policies.

Spam: Spam is unsolicited commercial e-mail. While many consider spam a trivial nuisance rather than an attack, it has been used as a means of enhancing malicious code attacks. The most significant consequence of spam, however, is the waste of computer and human resources. Many organizations attempt to cope with the flood of spam by using e-mail filtering technologies.

Sniffer: A program or device that can monitor data traveling over a network. Sniffers can be used both for legitimate network management functions and for stealing information. Unauthorized sniffers can be extremely dangerous to a network's security, because they are virtually impossible to detect and can be inserted almost anywhere. Sniffers often work on TCP/IP networks, where they sometimes are called packet sniffers. Sniffers add risk to the network, because many systems and users send information on local networks in clear text.

Pharming: Pharming is a cyber attack where a website traffic is redirected to another site and not to the intended site. These type of attacks are conducted by changing the host files on the attacked system or can make use of the various vulnerability holes in the DNS server and make large scale changes in the various entries. In either of these cases, the net result is that whenever a user tries to access a site which is under a pharming attack, the user will get redirected to another site which will most likely be a fake one.

Hacker tools: A hacking tool is a program or utility designed to help a hacker with hacking. It can also be proactively utilized to protect a network or computer from hackers. Hacking is intentional modification of computer software or hardware that is outside the architectural perimeters and design. A hacking tool is commonly used to gain unauthorized access to a PC to insert worms, sniffers, viruses and trojan horses. Some of the hacker tools can be described as follows.

- Nmap: Nmap ("Network Mapper") is a free open source utility for network exploration or security auditing. It was designed to rapidly scan large networks, although it works fine against single hosts. Nmap uses raw IP packets in novel ways to determine what hosts are available on the network, what services (application name and version) those hosts are offering, what operating systems (and OS versions) they are running, what type of packet filters/firewalls are in use, etc.

- Nessus remote security scanner: Works with a client-server framework. Nessus is the world's most popular vulnerability scanner used in over 75,000 organizations world-wide. Many of the world's largest organizations are realizing significant cost savings by using Nessus to audit business-critical enterprise devices and applications.

- John the Ripper: John the Ripper is a fast password cracker, currently available for many versions of Unix (11 are officially supported, not counting different architectures), DOS, Win32, BeOS, and OpenVMS. Its primary purpose is to detect weak Unix passwords.

- Nikto: Nikto is an Open Source (GPL) web server scanner which performs comprehensive tests against web servers for multiple items, including over 3200 potentially dangerous files/CGIs, versions on over 625 servers, and version specific problems on over 230 servers. Scan items and plugins are frequently updated and can be automatically updated

- SuperScan: Powerful TCP port scanner, pinger, resolver.

- P0f: P0f v2 is a versatile passive OS fingerprinting tool.

- Wireshark (formerly ethereal): Wireshark is a GTK+ based network protocol analyzer, or sniffer, that lets you capture and interactively browse the contents of network frames.

IAVA/Patching

The information assurance vulnerability alert (IAVA) is an announcement of an application software or operating system vulnerability notification in the form of alerts, bulletins, and technical advisories identified by DoD-CERT, a division of the United States Cyber Command. These elected vulnerabilities are the mandated baseline, or minimum configuration of all hosts residing on the GIG. USCYBERCOM analyzes each vulnerability and determines if it is necessary or beneficial to the Department of Defense to release it as an IAVA. Implementation of IAVA policy will help ensure that DoD components take appropriate mitigating actions against vulnerabilities to avoid serious compromises to DoD computer system assets that would potentially degrade mission performance.

Vulnerability management is a proactive approach to managing network security. It includes processes for:

- Checking for vulnerabilities: This process should include regular network scanning, logging, penetration testing use of an automated tool like a vulnerability scanner.
- Identifying vulnerabilities: This involves analyzing network scans and pen test results, firewall logs or vulnerability scan results to find anomalies that suggest malware attack or other malicious event has taken advantage of a security vulnerability, or could possibly do so.
- Verifying vulnerabilities: This process includes ascertaining whether the identified vulnerabilities could actually be exploited on servers, applications and networks or other systems. This also includes classifying the severity of a vulnerability and the level of risk it presents to the organization.

- Mitigating vulnerabilities: A process of identifying a software of its vulnerabilities by understanding the weaknesses and testing the software. This is a repeated process and is done until a solution is found. Often patch files may not be ready or patch files may not be available for the vulnerability. A vulnerability scanner is used to check for open ports or software which are likely to be susceptible to malware attacks. Vulnerabilities are corrected by changing the network policies or modifying the software or by adding patch files.
- Patching vulnerabilities: This is the process of getting patches, usually from the vendors of the affected software or hardware, and applying them to all the affected areas in a timely manner. This is sometimes an automated process, done with patch management tools. This step also includes patch testing.

SSL inspection: Secure Sockets Layer (SSL) is a cryptographic protocol that adds security to TCP/IP communication. Several versions of the SSL and transport layer security (TLS) protocols are in widespread use in applications like web browsing, electronic mail, internet faxing, instant messaging, and voice over IP (VoIP). SSL and TLS encrypt the transport layer protocol datagrams that carry the payload of these communications. While encryption is an excellent way to keep private data from prying eyes, without inspection by the IDP appliance, it also unwittingly opens a network to dangerous viruses, trojans, or network attacks.

Plain HTTP inspection: HTTP inspection allows admins to identify behavior and filter web traffic according to HTTP methods, URLs, and headers. It also allows admins to create filters or use default filters to identify web traffic. After the traffic is identified, IWSVA can control it according to policy settings that allow admins to determine the appropriate actions for specific traffic.

 Sample Test Questions

1) A random number that is associated with a user is added along with the password in each user accounts. This is most common among UNIX implementations.

   A) Hash
   B) Private Key
   C) Public Key
   D) SALT

The correct answer is D:) SALT. Salt is a random number associated with the user which will be added to the user's password when the hash is computes, and stores this SALT is used in most UNIX implementations.

2) A RFID or a proximity card is an example of _____ type of authentication category.

   A) Something you give
   B) Something you have
   C) Something you are
   D) Something you know

The correct answer is B:) Something you have. The authentication is done using something which is been carried along as an authentication device.

3) Which is a type of cryptographical scheme is employed in digital signatures?

   A) Symmetric
   B) Asymmetric
   C) Private key
   D) Substitution cipher

The correct answer is B:) Asymmetric. The digital signature schemes usually employs a type of PKI or asymmetric cryptography for its operation.

4) Authorization falls in the _____ phase of access control.

   A) Formulation
   B) Accounting
   C) Enforcement
   D) Initialization

The correct answer is A:) Formulating phase. Here the various permissions or privileges for different users are decided.

5) _____ is an authorization method that selects which authenticated users can access a particular resource.

   A) Apache require
   B) Active directory
   C) Digital signature
   D) Password

The correct answer is A:) Apache require. This is another authorization method that selects which authenticated users can access a particular resource.

6) _____ is a statement of the various procedures which a certification authority employs in issuing and managing certificates.

   A) RA
   B) CP
   C) CPS
   D) CRL

The correct answer is C:) CPS. A certification practice statement (CPS) is a statement of the practices which a certification authority employs in issuing and managing certificates.

7) A type of proximity card which is not powered and uses the RF energy from the requester to reply with whatever information is stored by the card

   A) Active RFID
   B) Passive RFID
   C) Magnetic strip card
   D) Crypto graphical calculator

The correct answer is B:) Passive RFID.

8) Open BSD is a type of password which uses _____ encryption.

   A) Symmetric
   B) Blowfish
   C) RSA
   D) Diffie Hellman

The correct answer is B:) Blowfish. OpenBSD does a hash based on blowfish encryption, and then stores the hashed password along with 128 bits of salt. The system guarantees that no two accounts will have the same salt value.

9) The password system used by Windows NT operating system stores two password hashes which are:

   A) LanMan and MD5 Hash
   B) LanMan and NT Hash
   C) NT Hash and Blowfish
   D) None of the above

The correct answer is B:) LanMan and NT Hash. Windows NT stores two password hashes: one called the LanMan hash and another called the NT hash.

10) In credit cards along with magnetic strip card is further authenticated by implementing _____ by keeping a 4 to 7 character pin.

   A) 2-Factor authentication
   B) 3-Factor authentication
   C) 4-Factor authentication
   D) None

The correct answer is A:) 2-Factor authentication. A credit card transaction lies in this category. Here the cards are further secured by implementing a 2-factor authentication by keeping a 4 to 7 character PIN whenever the card is used.

11) Proximity cards which falls in the category of _____ are powered and broadcast information, hence allowing anyone who is in the range and has a receiver to query the card.

   A) Active RFID
   B) Passive RFID
   C) Magnetic strip card
   D) Cryptographical calculator

The correct answer is A:) Active RFID. Active RFID is powered and hence broadcasts information, allowing anyone who is in range and has a receiver to query the card.

12) _____, _____, and _____ are the major characteristic of a strong password.

   A) Length, complexity, character set
   B) Complexity, randomness, abstraction
   C) Abstraction, length, randomness
   D) Length, character set, randomness

The correct answer is D:) Length, character set, randomness.

13) When an eavesdropper gains control of the secret key intercepted through the communication medium connected with the network. This password hacking is known as?

   A) Backdoor
   B) Teardrop
   C) Shoulder surfing
   D) Wire tapping

The correct answer is D:) Wire tapping. Wire tapping through which the secret key is intercepted through the wire used to send it to the machine.

14) A document can be digitally signed with _____ and can be verified using a _____ of the signed person.

   A) Private key, public key
   B) Public key, private key
   C) Secret salt, public key
   D) Public key, secret salt

The correct answer is A:) Private key, public key. Digital signatures are signed by the private key of the creator of the document, which is checked for genuineness by the receiver with the sender's public key.

15) In _____ administrators create a set of levels and each user is linked with a specific access level. The access is restricted for that user for all the resources that are greater than his access level.

   A) DAC
   B) MAC
   C) Both A & B
   D) None

The correct answer is B:) MAC. In MAC, administrators create a set of levels and each user is linked with a specific access level.

16) _____, _____ are examples of a symmetric key scheme.

   A) ECC, DES
   B) RSA, AES
   C) IDEA, RC4
   D) AES, ECC

The correct answer is A:) ECC, DES. Cryptographic algorithms like symmetric key (AES, DES, 3DES, IDEA, RC4) used for data confidentiality and integrity.

17) _____ is a security protocol suite used for network layer.

   A) IP Sec
   B) SSL/TLS
   C) IEEE 802.1x
   D) None

The correct answer is A:) IP Sec. The various security suites and standards for network layers includes IEEE 802.1x for Link Layer ensures authentication and access control. IPsec for network layer, and SSL/TLS for transport layer.

18) The first stage of the chain of evidence is?

   A) Preservation
   B) Collection
   C) Examination
   D) Analysis

The correct answer is A:) Preservation. Preservation involves operations that prevent or stop any activities that can damage the various digital information. This involves the various operations such as preventing people from using computers during collection, stopping ongoing deletion processes, and choosing the safest way to collect information.

19) The right to information or public access of information held by the public authorities is called

   A) Freedom of Information Act
   B) HIPAA
   C) Sarbanes Oxley
   D) US Patriot Act

The correct answer is A:) Freedom Of Information Act. The Freedom of Information Act of 2000 provides the public access to information held by public authorities.

20) Which of the following defines the safety of the commonwealth duty to our principals and to each other?

   A) Code of Ethics
   B) US Patriot Act
   C) HIPAA
   D) Principles of Information Security

The correct answer is A:) Code of Ethics. The rules that govern personal conduct are collectively known as rules of ethics. Security professionals should maintain high levels of ethics.

21) The freezing of all the activities including deleting of files, updating of databases as a part of investigation of a cyber crime comes under which stage of digital forensics?

   A) Preservation
   B) Collection
   C) Examination
   D) Analysis

The correct answer is A:) Preservation.

22) This provides law enforcement agencies with broader latitude in order to combat terrorism related activities

   A) US Patriot Act
   B) Freedom Of Information Act
   C) HIPAA
   D) Security Act

The correct answer is A:) US Patriot Act.

23) Which of the following protects from intellectual property?

   A) DMCA
   B) HIPAA
   C) Freedom Of Information Act
   D) RTI

The correct answer is A:) DMCA. The Digital Millennium Copyright Act (DMCA) is the American contribution to an international effort by the World Intellectual Properties Organization (WIPO) to reduce the impact of copyright, trademark, and privacy infringement, especially when accomplished via the removal of technological copyright protection measures.

24) This is an application level security protocol

   A) PGP
   B) AES
   C) SNMP
   D) CMAC

The correct answer is A:) PGP. The application security concerns includes protocols like SMTP/MIME for mail, PGP, HTTP and HTTPS.

25) A biometric system installed in your organization incorrectly matches a person's biometric pattern to the stored pattern in its database gives him an access. This type of error is known as

   A) Type 1 error
   B) Type 2 error
   C) Both A and B
   D) Authorization error

The correct answer is B:) Type 2 error.

26) An intruder gets an access to the server room by secretly following your system administrator with/without his knowledge. Such an intrusion can be named as

A) Barging in
B) Tailgating
C) Physical intrusion
D) Detective intrusion

The correct answer is B:) Tailgating. This is the most common type of the insider intruder attacks that can happen. People usually, knowingly or unknowingly, unlock the electronic gates and let the intruder get inside the restricted areas.

27) Which is a type of electronic locking system which when powered is locked?

A) Fail secure
B) Fail safe
C) Fail proof
D) Fail-when-powered

The correct answer is B:) Fail safe. Fail safe locks needs power to lock. When the power is interrupted by some access control mechanism or powers out break this is unlocked.

28) _____ is a system used in server rack to avoid overheating of processors. This is done by introducing hot air outlets and cold air intake in the server racks.

A) Hot and cold conditioning
B) Hot and cold aisles
C) Hot and cold waving
D) None

The correct answer is B:) Hot and cold aisles. The cooling systems used to prevent overheating in server racks are known as hot and cold aisles. The rows of servers in a server are cooled with hot aisles by introducing hot air outlets whereby cold aisles introduces cool air intake for cooling the equipment.

29) Backing up data files can be categorized into _____ security

   A) Environment security
   B) Preventive physical security
   C) Detective physical security
   D) Storage physical security

The correct answer is B:) Preventive physical security. Preventive physical controls prevent unauthorized access to vulnerable areas like the server room, data processing facilities and other important areas.

30) The observation that is taken by any Biometric System from a human is known as

   A) Biometric sense
   B) Biometric evidence
   C) Biometric signature
   D) Biometric foot print

The correct answer is C:) Biometric signature. The biometric sensor takes an observation depending up on its type. This is known as the biometric signature of that person.

31) _____ is the percentage of data input that is considered invalid and fails to input into the biometric system.

   A) FER
   B) FRR
   C) FAR
   D) None of the above

The correct answer is A:) FER. Failure to enroll happens when the data obtained by the sensor is considered invalid or of poor quality.

32) _____ is a media sanitation method performed by exposing the magnetic media to a strong magnetic field to disrupt the recorded magnetic domains.

   A) Purging
   B) Shredding
   C) Magnetizing
   D) Degaussing

The correct answer is D:) Degaussing. A degausser is a device that generates a magnetic field used to sanitize magnetic media.

33) _____ maintains record of system activity by system or application processes or by user initiated processes.

   A) Audit logs
   B) Config files
   C) Meta files
   D) System info

The correct answer is A:) Audit logs. An audit log is a full historic account of all events that are relevant for a certain object.

34) A hacker is trying to intrude and spy on your organizational network. What should be examined to detect this?

   A) Firewall system file
   B) Configuration file
   C) Antivirus scan results
   D) Audit logs

The correct answer is D:) Audit logs. An audit log is a full historic account of all events that are relevant for a certain object.

35) Instead of obtaining server and desktop licenses for software products it uses, an enterprise can obtain the same function through a hosted service through a network connection. This is called

   A) SaaS
   B) PaaS
   C) IaaS
   D) None

The correct answer is A:) SaaS. Software-as-a-service provides complete applications to a cloud's end user. This can be mainly accessed through a web portal and service oriented architectures based on web service technologies. Instead of obtaining desktop and server licenses for software products it uses, an enterprise can obtain the same functions through a hosted service from a provider through a network connection.

36) This cloud model offers various raw computing provisions, storage and network infrastructure where you can load your own software.

   A) PaaS
   B) SaaS
   C) IaaS
   D) None

The correct answer is C:) IaaS. In this model, providers offer various "raw" computing provisions, storage and network infrastructure where you can load your own software. In IaaS, scaling and elasticity is the customer's responsibility.

37) _____ is a deployment model of cloud where the infrastructure is shared by several firms that have a similar set of concerns in terms of security requirements, policies and target audience.

   A) Public cloud
   B) Hybrid cloud
   C) Community cloud
   D) Private cloud

The correct answer is C:) Community cloud. In a community cloud, the infrastructure is shared by several firms that have a similar set of concerns in terms of security requirements, policies, target audience, etc.

38) _____ is a categorization of cloud models in terms of availability they offer to their customers.

   A) Deployment models
   B) Employment models
   C) Service models
   D) Availability models

The correct answer is A:) Deployment models.

39) _____ is a point to point communication tunnel over an intermediary non-trusted network, mostly internet.

   A) ISDN
   B) VPN
   C) Firewall
   D) SSL/TLS

The correct answer is B:) VPN. Virtual Private Network is a point to point communication tunnel over an intermediary non-trusted network, mostly internet. Here proper authentication methods and strong encryption methods are used for protecting the encapsulated traffic.

40) Which of the following is NOT a VPN protocol?

   A) PPTP
   B) L2F
   C) L2TP
   D) PPP

The correct answer is D:) PPP. There are four common VPN protocols are PPTP, L2F, L2TP and IPSec.

41) _____ is a type of hypervisor.

   A) Mere-visor
   B) Bare-metal
   C) Bare-virtual
   D) None

The correct answer is B:) Bare-metal. A hypervisor can be of two types. Type I (bare-metal) or Type II (hosted).

42) Virtualization is made possible by using

   A) Hypervisor
   B) SSL/TLS
   C) Supervisor
   D) PPTP

The correct answer is A:) Hypervisor. Virtualization is made possible by abstracting the hardware and making it available to the virtual machines. This abstraction is usually done using a hypervisor.

43) _____ provides a complete system platform which supports the execution of a complete operating system in a cloud.

   A) Process virtual machine
   B) System virtual machine
   C) Programmable virtual machine
   D) None of the above

The correct answer is B:) System virtual machine. A system virtual machine provides a complete system platform which supports the execution of a complete operating system (OS).

44) _____ is a threat faced by cloud computing where a valid session key is used to gain unauthorized access for the information in a particular system.

   A) Session riding
   B) Session stealing
   C) Service hijacking
   D) Session dismissing

The correct answer is C:) Session hijacking. Session hijacking refers to use of a valid session key to gain unauthorized access for the information or services residing on a computer system, it also refers to theft of a cookie used to authenticate a user to a remote server.

45) Which of the following implies protecting information from disclosure from unauthorized parties?

   A) Confidentiality
   B) Integrity
   C) Availability
   D) None

The correct answer is A:) Confidentiality.

46) Which of the following is usually used for protecting the integrity of data?

   A) MD5
   B) RSA
   C) AES
   D) None

The correct answer is A:) MD5. The most commonly used methods to protect data integrity includes hashing the data you receive and comparing it with the hash of the original message.

47) _____ is an attack on the availability of data

   A) DDoS
   B) Trojan horse
   C) Man-in-the-middle
   D) Rootkit

The correct answer is A:) DDoS. Information only has value if the right people can access it at the right times.

48) _____ can be defined as a specific weakness in security.

   A) Threat
   B) Vulnerability
   C) Loopholes
   D) None

The correct answer is B:) Vulnerability. A vulnerability can be defined as a specific weakness in security (or a lack of security measures) that typically could be exploited by multiple adversaries having a range of motivations and interest in a lot of different assets.

49) The data servers do not have up-to-date virus definitions. This can be categorized as a

   A) Threat
   B) Vulnerability
   C) Risk
   D) Loophole

The correct answer is B:) Vulnerability. A vulnerability can be defined as a specific weakness in security (or a lack of security measures) that typically could be exploited by multiple adversaries having a range of motivations and interest in a lot of different assets.

50) _____ are disaster recovery sites with all necessary equipments, personnel, and software which are ready to be shifted without a moment's notice in case of failure/break down of main site.

   A) Hot sites
   B) Cold sites
   C) Warm sites
   D) Red hot sites

The correct answer is A:) The hot sites are disaster recovery sites with all necessary equipment, personnel, software and ready to be shifted without a moment's notice in case of failure/ breakdown of main site.

51) _____ in SSL is used as a secured transport service.

   A) Change cipher protocol
   B) Alert protocol
   C) Handshake protocol
   D) TLS protocol

The correct answer is A:) Change cipher protocol.

52) _____ is one among the deliverable of initialization phase of SDLC.

- A) Cost benefit analysis
- B) System test plans
- C) Test data development
- D) None of the above

The correct answer is A:) Cost benefit analysis. This phase comprises of requirement gathering and analysis.

53) The security measure that can be taken in the maintenance phase is

- A) Performing backups
- B) Developing test data
- C) Receiving volume projections
- D) Risk assessments

The correct answer is A:) Performing backups. Maintenance phase deals with the various enhancements and up gradations of the system. The primary concern of this phase is system availability.

54) SSL protocol has how many layers?

- A) One layer
- B) Two layers
- C) Three layers
- D) Four layers

The correct answer is B:) Two layers. SSL/TLS contains two layers of protocols.

55) _____ is a secure method of file transfer.

- A) FTP
- B) SFTP
- C) FSTP
- D) FTP-Secure

The correct answer is B:) SFTP. Secure File Transfer Protocol (SFTP) offers a more secure way to transfer files. SFTP is usually built upon Secure Shell (SSH) and is able to encrypt commands and data transfers over a network, thereby reducing the likelihood of interception attacks.

56) What is the underlying protocol of secure file transfer?

   A) SSL/TLS
   B) IPSec
   C) L2F
   D) PPTP

The correct answer is A:) SSL/TLS. Secure Sockets Layer/Transport Layer Security (SSL/TLS) can be used as the underlying protocol for SFTP. Like SSH, SSL/TLS authenticates the identity of both the server and the client, as well as encrypts communications between the two.

57) Which of the following is a bit of additional information added either to the TCP or UDP?

   A) IP address
   B) Port address
   C) Socket address
   D) None

The correct answer is B:) Port address. Ports are special addresses that allow communication between hosts. Ports identify how a communication process occurs. A port number is added from the source, indicating which port to communicate with on a server.

58) Which port is commonly used for running the service echo?

   A) Port No 4
   B) Port No 7
   C) Port No 11
   D) Port No 12

The correct answer is B:) Port No 7. This port is commonly used for running the service echo. Echo is an out dated service that echoes whatever is sent to it. This is often used in DoS attacks.

59) Which port is used to run the service trivial file transfer protocol?

　　A) Port 21
　　B) Port 23
　　C) Port 69
　　D) Port 67

The correct answer is C:) Port 69.

60) _____ runs the service SOCKS

　　A) Port 0
　　B) Port 312
　　C) Port 513
　　D) Port 1080

The correct answer is D:) Port 1080. This protocol tunnels traffic through firewalls, allowing many people behind the firewall to access the internet through a single IP address.

61) _____ phase in network scanning which creates the profile of the target organization, with the basic information such as its DNS and IP address.

　　A) Foot printing
　　B) Scanning
　　C) Enumeration
　　D) None of these

The correct answer is A:) Foot printing. This phase creates the profile of the target organization, with the basic information such as its domain name system (DNS) and e-mail servers, and its IP address range.

62) Which of the following is an area of network management that handles the proper operation of each component individually and with each other to find out the bugs?

　　A) Configuration management
　　B) Fault management
　　C) Performance management
　　D) Security management

The correct answer is B:) Fault management. Every effective fault management system have majorly two subsystems: reactive fault management and proactive fault management.

63) Which protocol is in charge of network management?

A) SMTP
B) MIME
C) SNMP
D) POP

The correct answer is C:) SNMP. The basic frame work for managing the network components in an internet is provided by SNMP - Simple Network Management Protocol. SNMP uses the concept of manager and agent where the manager is usually the host that controls and monitors a group of agents, usually routers. SNMP is an application level protocol.

64) Which of the following is a method of data hiding where a message is kept hidden in a picture?

A) Steganography
B) Cryptography
C) Bitmap
D) Pictography

The correct answer is A:) Steganography. This data then can be decoded using some effective algorithms at the receiving end.

65) Which is a hash function named after the first galaxy recognized to have a spiral structure?

A) Whirlpool
B) Milkyway
C) MD5
D) SHA

The correct answer is A:) Whirlpool. Whirlpool is a relatively recent cryptographic hash function that has received international recognition and adoption by standards organizations, including the International Organization for Standardization (ISO). Named after the first galaxy recognized to have a spiral structure, it creates a hash of 512 bits. Whirlpool is being implemented in several new commercial cryptography applications.

66) _____ is a block cipher which divides plaintext into 64-bit blocks and then executes the algorithm 16 times.

A) DES
B) AES
C) 3DES
D) MD5

The correct answer is A:) DES. It divides plaintext into 64-bit blocks and then executes the algorithm 16 times. There are four modes of DES encryption. Although DES was once widely implemented, its 56-bit key is no longer considered secure and has been broken several times. It is not recommended for use.

67) Which is used to strengthen WEP encryption?

A) WAP
B) WAP2
C) TKIP
D) SHA

The correct answer is C:) TKIP. To strengthen WEP encryption, a temporal key integrity protocol (TKIP) was employed. This placed a 128-bit wrapper around the WEP encryption with a key that is based on things such as the MAC address of the destination device and the serial number of the packet. TKIP was designed as a backward-compatible replacement to WEP, and it could work with all existing hardware.

68) Which refers to travelling around the town with a laptop looking for APs to connect with?

A) War driving
B) Access driving
C) War chalking
D) Access wandering

The correct answer is A:) War driving. The network card on the intruder's laptop is set to promiscuous mode, and it looks for signals coming from anywhere. After intruders gain access, they may steal internet access or corrupt data.

69) _____ involves those who discover a way into the network leaving signals on, or outside the premise to notify others that a vulnerability exists there.

A) War chalking
B) Foot printing
C) War piloting
D) None

The correct answer is A:) War chalking. Once weaknesses have been discovered in a wireless network, war chalking can occur. War chalking involves those who discover a way into the network leaving signals (often written in chalk) on, or outside, the premise to notify others that a vulnerability exists there.

70) In WPA2, CCMP uses a _____ with a 48 bit initialization.

A) 64 bit DES
B) 128 bit AES
C) SHA
D) RSA

The correct answer is B:) 128 bit AES. WPA2 requires counter mode with cipher block chaining message authentication code protocol (CCMP). CCMP uses 128-bit AES encryption with a 48-bit initialization vector. The larger initialization vector in WPA2, increases the difficulty in cracking and minimizes the risk of a replay attack.

71) Proxy firewall filters at _____ layer

A) Network layer
B) Application layer
C) Virtual layer
D) Physical layer

The correct answer is B:) Application layer. A proxy firewall is able to open an incoming packet at the application level and find out whether that packet is legitimate or not. If the packet is legitimate, the firewall sends the message to the real server or else that packet is dropped.

72) Which intrusion detection system starts off with a database of known attacks and is capable of recognizing those attacks?

A) Behavior based
B) Signature based
C) Database based
D) Network based

The correct answer is B:) Signature based. IDS/IPS starts off with a database of known attacks and is capable of recognizing those attacks. The only negative point is that if the attack that is occurring is not in the database of signatures, then it won't be recognized by a purely signature-based IDS/IPS.

73) _____ enforces a pre-programmed security policy unilaterally across more than just packet header information.

A) Network based IDS
B) Next generation firewall
C) Host based firewall
D) None

The correct answer is B:) Next generation firewall. This can make a single device act as both a traditional Firewall and IPS.

74) _____ can be defined as a device or an application that analyzes whole packets, both header and payload, looking for known events. When an unknown event is detected, the packet is rejected.

A) IPS
B) IDS
C) Firewall
D) VPN

The correct answer is A:) IPS.

75) Which is an ethical hacker testing the state of the network at a particular point of time?

   A) Penetration testing
   B) Unit testing
   C) Vulnerability testing
   D) Focused testing

The correct answer is A:) Penetration testing. This will help them to discover the various vulnerabilities of their networks and also uncover any areas which a real hacker can get an undue advantage on the network.

76) Which wireless access points in the network will not give the alert to the admin if connected to?

   A) Silent access points
   B) Resilient access points
   C) Rouge access points
   D) Hidden access points

The correct answer is C:) Rouge access points.

77) _____ is the action of making something look like something that it is not in order to gain unauthorized access to a user's private information.

   A) Spoofing
   B) Smurfing
   C) Teardrops
   D) Rootkits

The correct answer is A:) Spoofing. The idea of spoofing originated in the 1980s with the discovery of a security hole in the TCP protocol.

78) _____ attacks overflow network traffic which is a kind of DoS where with the help of spoofed broadcast ping messages flooding of target system is done.

A) Spoofing
B) Smurfing
C) Teardrops
D) Cross site scripting

The correct answer is B:) Smurfing. The attacks through internet control message protocol (ICMP) messages, are known as a smurf attack. Smurf attack overflows network traffic which is a kind of denial of service attack where with the help of spoofed broadcast ping messages flooding of target system is done.

79) Usually smurf attacks make use of _____ and _____.

A) TCP and IP
B) IP and ICMP
C) IP and port numbers
D) TCP and MIME

The correct answer is B:) IP and ICMP.

80) In a _____ attack, huge amounts of messages are sent to a single node from multiple sources to run out the system resources, resulting in business system failure.

A) DoS
B) DDoS
C) Spoofing
D) Rootkit attack

The correct answer is B:) DDoS. Network packets use TCP/IP for transmission. The packets themselves are harmless, but if there are too many abnormal packets, it will cause the network devices or servers to overload. This can quickly consume the system resources. Another case is if the packets take advantage of certain protocol's defects (e.g. artificial incompleteness or malformation), causing the failure of network devices or servers. Both cases will result in denial of service.

81) _____ based DDoS attacks send mass junk data messages to cause overload to the depletion of network bandwidth or equipment resources.

   A) Bandwidth
   B) Application
   C) Communication
   D) Message

The correct answer is A:) Bandwidth. DDoS attacks of this type send mass junk data messages to cause an overload, leading to the depletion of network bandwidth or equipment resources.

82) Name the attack in which with DNS spoofing the DNS server is given information about a name server that it thinks is.

   A) Smurfing
   B) DDoS
   C) Teardrop
   D) DNS poisoning

The correct answer is D:) DNS poisoning.

83) _____ is a program which exploits an overlapping IP fragment bug present in WIN95/Win NT and WIN 3.1 machines.

   A) Spoofing
   B) Smurfing
   C) Teardrop
   D) CrossScripting

The correct answer is C:) Teardrop.

84) Which of the following steals the client cookies or any other sensitive information which can identify the client with the website?

   A) CSS script
   B) DDoS
   C) Teardrop
   D) DNS poisoning

The correct answer is A:) CSS script. Cross site scripting (CSS for short, but sometimes abbreviated as XSS) is one of the most common application level attacks that hackers use to sneak into web applications today. Cross site scripting is an attack on the privacy of clients of a particular web site which can lead to a total breach of security when customer details are stolen or manipulated.

85) Which is a computer program designed to provide continued privileged access to a computer while actively hiding its presence?

   A) Rootkit
   B) CSS script
   C) Teardrop
   D) DNS poisoning

The correct answer is A:) Rootkit. A rootkit is a computer program designed to provide continued privileged access to a computer while actively hiding its presence. A rootkit allows someone to maintain command and control over a computer without the computer user/owner knowing about it.

86) _____ manipulates the data base code to take advantage of a weakness of it.

   A) CSS script
   B) SQL injection
   C) Rootkit
   D) DBMS poisoning

The correct answer is B:) SQL injection. SQL (Structured Query Language) is used for communicating with online (and other relational) databases. With a SQL injection attack (also known as a SQL insertion attack), an attacker manipulates the database code to take advantage of a weakness in it.

87) _____ are maintenance hooks constructed deliberately by the developers while developing and testing an application which later remains open unnoticed by the programmers.

    A) Back door
    B) Tunnel
    C) Secret path
    D) None

The correct answer is A:) Back door. The term back door attack can have two different meanings. The original term back door referred to troubleshooting and developer hooks into systems that often circumvented normal authentication.

88) Which attack is an attempt to guess passwords until a successful guess occurs?

    A) Brute force
    B) Back door
    C) Password smurf
    D) None

The correct answer is A:) Brute force. A brute-force attack is an attempt to guess passwords until a successful guess occurs. Because of the nature of this routine, this type of attack usually occurs over a long period of time.

89) Which is an unsolicited commercial emailing technique?

    A) Spamming
    B) Phishing
    C) Sniffing
    D) Pharming

The correct answer is A:) Spamming. Spam is unsolicited commercial e-mail. While many consider spam a trivial nuisance rather than an attack, it has been used as a means of enhancing malicious code attacks.

90) _____ is a program or a device that can monitor data travelling over a network.

   A) Sniffer
   B) Smurfer
   C) Spammer
   D) None

The correct answer is A:) Sniffer. Sniffers can be used both for legitimate network management functions and for stealing information.

91) _____ can be accomplished by changing entries in the host file and on a large scale by changing entries in a DNS server.

   A) Pharming
   B) Spamming
   C) Phishing
   D) Cross Scripting

The correct answer is A:) Pharming.

92) _____ is the fastest password cracker, a hacker tool available in market.

   A) Nmap
   B) Nessus
   C) John the Ripper
   D) Nikto

The correct answer is C:) John the Ripper.

93) Which is a hacker tool which is a free open source utility for network exploration or security auditing?

   A) Nmap
   B) Nessus
   C) Nikto
   D) John the Ripper

The correct answer is A:) Nmap. Nmap (network mapper) is a free open source utility for network exploration or security auditing. It was designed to rapidly scan large networks, although it works fine against single hosts.

94) Which of the following is a hacker tool that is used known as the best vulnerability scanner?

   A) Nmap
   B) Nessus
   C) Nikto
   D) John the Ripper

The correct answer is B:) Nessus. This works with a client-server framework. Nessus is the world's most popular vulnerability scanner used in over 75,000 organizations world-wide.

95) _____ is a versatile passive OS finger printing tool.

   A) P0f
   B) Wireshark
   C) Nikto
   D) Nmap

The correct answer is A:) P0f.

96) Which of the following is a GTK+ based network protocol analyzer that interactively browse the contents of network frames?

   A) P0f
   B) Wireshark
   C) Nikto
   D) Superscan

The correct answer is B:) Wireshark.

97) Which of the following allows admins to identify behavior and filter the web traffic according to the header, URL?

   A) HTTP inspection
   B) SSL inspection
   C) TCP/IP inspection
   D) Port scanning

The correct answer is A:) HTTP inspection.

98) Which of the following is a cheap alternative of penetration testing arranges a large number of security researchers to hack a system and paying reward for any vulnerabilities found?

A) Big bounty programs
B) Automated penetration testing
C) Port scanning
D) Crowd sourcing

The correct answer is A:) Big bounty programs.

99) _____ is an act of altering the header of an email so that the email appears to be sent from someone else.

A) Email spoofing
B) Email smurfing
C) Email pharming
D) Email sniffing

The correct answer is A:) Email spoofing.

100) Which of the following is NOT part of a DDoDs attack?

A) Intermediary site is to be identified by attacker which helps in amplifying attack.
B) Large amount of traffic will be sent by attacker to the broadcast address at particular intermediary sites.
C) Intermediaries will provide broadcast to all hosts which are there in a subnet.
D) All of the above.

The correct answer is D:) All of the above. None of these steps are part of a DDoDs attack. These are the steps in a smurf attack.

 ## Test Taking Strategies

Here are some test-taking strategies that are specific to this test and to other DSST tests in general:

- Keep your eyes on the time. Pay attention to how much time you have left.
- Read the entire question and read all the answers. Many questions are not as hard to answer as they may seem. Sometimes, a difficult sounding question really only is asking you how to read an accompanying chart. Chart and graph questions are on most DANTES/DSST tests and should be an easy free point.
- If you don't know the answer immediately, the new computer-based testing lets you mark questions and come back to them later if you have time.
- Read the wording carefully. Some words can give you hints to the right answer. There are no exceptions to an answer when there are words in the question such as always, all or none. If one of the answer choices includes most or some of the right answers, but not all, then that is not the answer. Here is an example:

    The primary colors include all of the following:
    A) Red, Yellow, Blue, Green
    B) Red, Green, Yellow
    C) Red, Orange, Yellow
    D) Red, Yellow, Blue

    Although item A includes all the right answers, it also includes an incorrect answer, making it incorrect. If you didn't read it carefully, were in a hurry, or didn't know the material well, you might fall for this.

- Make a guess on a question that you do not know the answer to. There is no penalty for an incorrect answer. Eliminate the answer choices that you know are incorrect. For example, this will let your guess be a 1 in 3 chance instead.

Legal Note

All rights reserved. This Study Guide, Book and Flashcards are protected under US Copyright Law. No part of this book or study guide or flashcards may be reproduced, distributed or stored in a retrieval system, or transmitted in any form or by any means, electronic, mechanical, photocopying, recording, or otherwise, without the prior written permission of the publisher Breely Crush Publishing, LLC.

DSST is a registered trademark of The Thomson Corporation and its affiliated companies, and does not endorse this book.

FLASHCARDS

This section contains flashcards for you to use to further your understanding of the material and test yourself on important concepts, names or dates. Read the term or question then flip the page over to check the answer on the back. Keep in mind that this information may not be covered in the text of the study guide. Take your time to study the flashcards, you will need to know and understand these concepts to pass the test.

Alert protocol	Asymmetric key cryptosystems
Availability of information	Biometrics
Brute force	CA
Change cipher spec protocol	Cold sites

Uses two different key cryptosystems.	Used to convey SSL-related alerts to the peer entity.
Authentication systems based on the biological traits or the physical and behavioral properties you possess.	Ensuring that authorized parties are able to access the information when needed.
Certificate authority	An attempt to guess passwords until a successful guess occurs.
Sites which are basic with just power and connections.	Updates the cipher suite to be used on SSL connection.

Confidentiality of information	Cryptography
CSS	Data at rest
DDoS	DDoS attack
DMCA	Espionage

Uses algorithms to encrypt data and make it scrambled so that it cannot be readable by unauthorized users.	Protecting the information from disclosure to unauthorized parties.
Stored data	Cross site scripting
Huge amounts of messages are sent to a single node from multiple sources to run out the system resources, resulting in business system failure.	Distributed denial of service
Unauthorized access or data collection.	Digital Millennium Copyright Act

Forces of nature	FTP
Handshake protocol	HIPAA
Hoaxes	Hot sites
HTTP	Integrity of information

File transfer protocol	Fire, flood, earthquake, or lightening.
Health Insurance Portability and Accountability Act	The most complex part of SSL and is used as a secured transport service.
Disaster recovery sites with all necessary equipment, personnel, software and ready to be shifted without a moment's notice in case of failure/breakdown of the main site.	Trying to deceive the user into giving information to a (false) trusted source.
Protecting information from being modified by unauthorized parties.	Hypertext transfer protocol

IPS	L2TP
MAC	Next generation firewall
Nmap	Penetration testing
Pharming	PPTP

Layer 2 tunneling protocol	A device or an application that analyzes whole packets, both header and payload, looking for known events.
Enforces a pre-programmed security policy unilaterally across more than just packet header information.	Mandatory access control
An ethical hacker testing the state of the network at a particular point of time.	A hacker tool which is a free open source utility for network exploration or security auditing.
Point-to-point tunneling protocol	Cyber attack where a website traffic is redirected to another site and not to the intended site.

Risk management	Rouge access points
Sarbanes-Oxley	Session hijacking
SFTP	Sniffer
SQL	SQL injection

Wireless access points in the network will not give the alert to the admin if connected to.	Includes all those practices attempting to minimize security hazards by deciding intelligently how to deploy, modify, or reassign security resources.
Use of a valid session key to gain unauthorized access for the information or services residing on a computer system.	Improves the reliability and accuracy of financial reporting while increasing the accountability of corporate governance.
A program or device that can monitor data traveling over a network.	Secure file transfer protocol
Manipulates the data base code to take advantage of a weakness of it.	Structured query language

SSH	SSL/TLS
Symmetric key crytosystems	VM
VPN	Vulnerability assessment
Warm sites	Wireshark

Secure sockets layer/ transport layer security	Secure shell
Virtual machine	Uses the same key to encrypt and decrypt the moving data.
A practice that is executed attempting to discover security vulnerabilities that could be exploited by an intruder.	Virtual private network
A GTK+ based network protocol analyzer that interactively browse the contents of network frames.	A middle ground between hot and cold sites.

Threat assessment	Attack
Transit data	Proximity card or RFID
Digital signature	Key generation algorithm
Signing algorithm	Signature verifying algorithm

An attempt by an adversary to cause harm to valuable assets, usually by trying to exploit one or more vulnerabilities. The harm may include theft, sabotage, destruction, espionage, tampering, or adulteration.	This is the assessment done, as an attempt to predict possible threats. This may involve using intelligence data and information on past security incidents.
These cards transmit stored information to a monitor via RF.	Data which is transferred from one location to another.
An algorithm that selects a private key uniformly at random from a set of possible private keys. This algorithm outputs the private key and a corresponding public key.	An authentication system used to authenticate a digital message or document.
An algorithm that, given a message, public key and a signature, either accepts or rejects the message's claim to authenticity.	An algorithm that produces a signature with the given message and a private key.

RA	Repository
CPS	CP
Security architecture	Security domain
Freedom of Information Act	USA Patriot Act

An electronic certificate database that is available online	Registration authority
Certificate policy	Certification practice statement
The domain of all the layers of OSI which is a set of network, physical and logical elements protected by the security architecture.	The high level design that gives the structure of the system, which includes identifying main system components, the various defensive measures, and also their secure interconnections.
Provides law enforcement agencies with broader latitude in order to combat terrorism-related activities.	Provides the public access to information held by public authorities.

Audit log	**Session riding**
Ports	**Network scanning**
Network management and analysis	**Steganography**
Hash algorithm	**Symmetric algorithm**

Refers to the hackers sending commands to a web application on behalf of the targeted user by just sending that user an email or tricking the user into visiting a specially crafted website.	A full historic account of all events that are relevant for a certain object.
A procedure for identifying active hosts in a network, either for the purpose of attacking them or for network security assessment.	Special addresses that allow communication between hosts.
Another method of message hiding, in which the message or the data that should be kept secure is hidden inside an image. This data then can be decoded using some effective algorithms at the receiving end.	A function that initializes, monitors, tests, configures, modifies and trouble shoots the operations of network components so that the entire network meets the expectations of the organization.
Uses the same shared single key to encrypt and decrypt a document.	The most basic type of cryptographic algorithm, a process for creating a unique digital fingerprint for a set of data.

WEP	Firewall
FAR	CER
Media management	Shielding
Tailgating	Spoofing

A device installed between the internal network of an organization and the rest of the internet.	Wired equivalent privacy
Crossover error rate	False acceptance rate
A process of armoring computer systems to prevent an intelligent intruder to decode information from the electronic emissions from the system.	The various steps that should be taken care of in order to protect media and the data it contains.
The action of making something look like something that it is not in order to gain unauthorized access to a user's private information.	The method of getting entry to electronically locked rooms or buildings by following someone through the door they just unlocked.

NOTES

NOTES